Mystics in Action

MYSTICS IN ACTION

Twelve Saints for Today

BRUCE G. EPPERLY

ORBIS BOOKS
Maryknoll, New York 10545

Founded in 1970, Orbis Books endeavors to publish works that enlighten the mind, nourish the spirit, and challenge the conscience. The publishing arm of the Maryknoll Fathers and Brothers, Orbis seeks to explore the global dimensions of the Christian faith and mission, to invite dialogue with diverse cultures and religious traditions, and to serve the cause of reconciliation and peace. The books published reflect the views of their authors and do not represent the official position of the Maryknoll Society. To learn more about Orbis Books, please visit our website at www.orbisbooks.com.

Copyright © 2020 by Bruce G. Epperly

Published by Orbis Books, Box 302, Maryknoll, NY 10545-0302.

Manufactured in the United States of America

Library of Congress Cataloging-in-Publication Data

Names: Epperly, Bruce Gordon, author.
Title: Mystics in action : twelve saints for today / Bruce G. Epperly.
Description: Maryknoll, NY : Orbis Books, 2020. | Includes
    bibliographical references and index. | Summary: Portrays the lives
    and experiences of twelve mystical activists, exploring their
    worldview and spirituality and their relationship to social
    transformation
Identifiers: LCCN 2020021057 (print) | LCCN 2020021058 (ebook)
    | ISBN 9781626983892 (trade paperback) | ISBN 9781608338535
    (epub)
Subjects: LCSH: Mystics—Biography.
Classification: LCC BV5095.A1 E66 2020 (print) | LCC BV5095.A1
    (ebook) | DDC 270.8092/2 [B]—dc23
LC record available at https://lccn.loc.gov/2020021057
LC ebook record available at https://lccn.loc.gov/2020021058

Contents

Acknowledgments

The philosopher Alfred North Whitehead once noted that the whole universe conspires to create each moment of experience. Whitehead's affirmation describes the creative process embodied in relationships that gave birth to this text. I am grateful to South Congregational Church, Centerville, Massachusetts, which sponsored the "Month with a Mystic" series from which this book emerged. The mystics described in this book came alive in conversation with seminar participants. I wish to thank the spiritual guides whose wisdom across the centuries has shaped my spiritual journey, most especially Howard Thurman, Abraham Joshua Heschel, the Desert Mothers and Fathers, and the Celtic Adventurers. The deep spirituality of Georgetown University colleagues and spiritual companions Rev. Johanna Newberry Green and Rabbi Harold Saul White lives on in my own mystical journey. For over forty years, Kate Epperly has been my companion in marriage, parenting, grandparenting, and spirituality. It was a wondrous gift to work with my editor, Jill Brennan O'Brien, once a student, now a friend and colleague, whose care has added zest to this text. In the spirit of *ubuntu*, I say to all of these, and many more, "I am because of you."

INTRODUCTION

Heavenly Minded and Earthly Good: The *Mystic as Activist*

When I was a child, some of the saints of our Bible-believing church were described by the expression "they're so heavenly minded that they're no earthly good." These faithful souls were so wrapped up in their piety that they were unable to perform the ordinary tasks of life. Heaven was their destination, and they had little interest in the realities of domestic life and civic responsibility. They saw this-worldly responsibilities as of little importance compared to the promises of eternal life. These neighborhood saints were so heavenly minded they had difficulty balancing a checkbook, getting to work on time, or pumping gas! Civic responsibility was shunned as irrelevant. After all, they believed, if you have enough faith, Jesus will take care of everything!

This same stereotypical description is also invoked to describe mystics. Mysticism is perceived to be in opposition to concern for social justice and civic involvement. Mystics are believed to be persons whose encounters with God lead them away from everyday life, rendering them virtually useless to neighbors in need. According to many observers, things of the earth are of little consequence as these spiritual pilgrims immerse themselves in monastic solitude and introspection, constantly checking the temperature of their inner lives and giving little thought to the winds of change gusting around them. Given this perception, some congregations struggle to find their focus: Should they be prayerful and contemplative or activist and political?

This perceived dualism of contemplation and activism does not apply to the mystics described in this text. These heavenly minded seekers were also activists whose feet were firmly planted on the ground in their concern for justice, equality, and care for the earth. Their quest for God inspired solidarity with those who suffer injustice and exclusion. These mystics, such as Thomas Merton, who spent much of his adult life in the solitude and silence of a Trappist monastery, realized that despite their apparent distance from the halls of power, they—along with the rest of us—are guilty bystanders who have a responsibility to promote the well-being of the institutions and communities that shape the lives of our human and nonhuman companions. Even in solitude, we cannot escape the deafening realities of war, racial injustice, sexual discrimination, refugees and immigration, and planetary destruction. Doing nothing and turning away from the world makes us complicit in the evils we abhor. Others, such as Mother Teresa, see God's presence in all persons and then plunge into the world of the suffering, providing comfort and dignity to outcasts dying on the street, and simply seeking to do something beautiful for God in every encounter. They recognize that God hears the cries of the poor. Our care for the least of these is our gift to God. Still others, such as Albert Schweitzer, leave the ivory tower and concert hall, motivated by the quest to pursue the dream of Shalom, thus embodying in service to the vulnerable the ministry of Jesus. For these mystical spirits, the God found in silence and solitude is equally present in crusading for workers' rights, comforting the dying, marching for civil rights, and picketing for peace.

To these heavenly minded souls, spiritual transformation emerges from hours spent in prayer and meditation. These often-solitary practices are intended to expand, rather than diminish, our sensitivity to the suffering around us, much of which is caused by institutional decision making and societal values. In the spirit of Jesus's own spiritual sensitivities, growing in wisdom and stature awakens us to the cries of the poor and the voices of the voiceless. Time in meditation is an inspiration to see traces of God in all things and a catalyst to become God's companions in healing the world.

Mysticism expands our scope of concern. Activist mystics seek to be both heavenly minded and earthly good. They cannot turn away from the world's suffering but must provide a healing balm to ease the pain and prevent future agony. They see their vocation as tearing down the walls that prevent people from experiencing the fullness of divine blessing, transforming both souls and social structures.

While there is no uniformity in mystical experience or spiritual practice, the mystics described in this text understood mysticism as ultimately a relational, loving response to God, whose love for them and the world inspires them to claim their vocation of being God's companions in healing the earth. God's love for us encourages us to become channels of love to the world. These mystics inspire a twenty-first-century vision of spiritual transformation, this-worldly in focus and committed to experiencing God's presence in the maelstrom of political, relational, and economic conflict. This "affirmative mysticism," to coin a phrase from Rufus Jones, takes the world seriously because God takes the world seriously. The traditional doctrines of divine omnipresence and omniscience mean what they say: God is present everywhere and can be experienced in both meditation hall and picket line. They also affirm that God shows up wherever there is suffering. God is not aloof or apathetic. God experiences our world, not in an eternal, unchanging vision, but in the unfolding of history in all its ambiguity, wonder, and pain. The divine pathos, God's full-hearted experience of our lives, as described by Abraham Joshua Heschel, finds its embodiment in the streets of Calcutta, marching against racial injustice in Selma, working for peace in the United Nations, challenging the military-industrial complex at a munitions plant, protesting for fair wages and workers' rights on a picket line, and working secretly to overthrow dictators. As Dietrich Bonhoeffer asserts, "only a suffering God can help," and God needs our help to ease to the pain of our brothers and sisters in the human and nonhuman world.

Dorothee Soelle affirms that "We are all mystics," and I believe she is right.[1] Such pronouncements may seem unrealistic, given our preoccupations with the complexities of work and domestic life, the dramas of our own little worlds, and the anxiety-provoking machinations of political leaders. Yet, moving within our daily tasks and civic responsibilities, divine wisdom can be experienced, if we pause long enough to notice it.

The divine call may come as a result of preparation through spiritual practices. It may also come unexpectedly as it came to Isaiah at the Jerusalem Temple (Isa 6:1–8) or in a professional and spiritual crisis as it came to Martin Luther King Jr. in the kitchen of his home. In claiming our relationship with God as the center of our lives, new energies of self-awareness and new possibilities for social transformation emerge. We may even discover that our day-to-day callings of work, parenting, and family life, as well as our social and interpersonal involvements, can be our platform, as Mother Teresa (now Saint Teresa) of Calcutta counsels, for doing "something beautiful for God."

In describing the relationship between mysticism and social concern, African American spiritual guide Howard Thurman notes the holistic character of our encounters with God:

> For our purposes, then, mysticism is defined as the response of the individual to a personal encounter with God within his own soul. . . . Such a response is total,

---

1. Dorothee Soelle, *The Silent Cry: Mysticism and Resistance* (Minneapolis: Augsburg Fortress, 2001), 9.

effecting the inner quality of the [mystic's] life and its outward expression as its manifestation.[2]

Our inner life must be embodied in our interpersonal relations and political involvements. Jesus goes to the wilderness to
discern his vocation, face the temptations of spiritual power, and
then returns to the world as God's messenger of Shalom. Dietrich
Bonhoeffer's encounters with the living God in scripture and sacrament compel him to confront the diabolical machinations of his
nation's leaders. Our encounters with God inspire us to personal
and social transformation and sensitize us to institutionally based
impediments to experiencing the Reality that has become central
to our lives. As Thurman notes, the mystic commits him- or herself to "the removal of all that prevents God from coming to himself in the life of the individual. Whatever there is that blocks this,
calls for action."[3] Although the mystic may be personally oriented
toward prayer and meditation, the encounter with God is a process of immersion, not escape, widening the heart to experience
the suffering of persons who are poor, marginalized, ostracized,
and oppressed. "Social action, therefore, is an expression of resistance against whatever tends to, or separates one from, the experience of God, who is the very ground of his being."[4]

We are in desperate need of mystics for our time. We need
this-worldly mystics whose spiritual practices interface with the
24/7 "breaking news" cycle, the immediacy of tragedies across the
globe, the bloviation of polarizing politicians, the tragedy of school
shootings, the rise in hate crimes and incivility, and the reality of
climate change. Mystic visions are catalysts for experiencing God ·
in all things and then awakening all things to God's compassion-

2. Howard Thurman, *Mysticism and Social Action: Lawrence Lectures
and Discussions with Dr. Howard Thurman* (London: International
Association for Religious Freedom, 2014), Kindle location, 177–79.

3. Ibid., Kindle location, 244–45.

4. Ibid., Kindle location, 235–36.

ate and healing presence, letting their inner light become a force for social enlightenment.

There are many ways to describe the mystic's journey. In her classic on mysticism, Evelyn Underhill portrays the journey to God as a process involving awakening, purgation, illumination, the dark night, and union. Theologian and spiritual guide Matthew Fox speaks of spiritual experience in terms of the four ways of mystical adventure: the way of wonder (*via positiva*), the way of suffering and simplicity (*via negativa*), the way of creativity and agency (*via creativa*), and the way of transformation *(via transformativa)*. Beginning with the original wholeness of creation and human life, Fox sees the mystic path as profoundly relational and transformational in its integration of personal growth and social responsibility. The transpersonal nature of mystical experiences finds its fulfillment in facing the challenges of daily life, political involvement, and care for the planet. While Underhill represents a more traditional description of the mystic's path, she too recognizes that mysticism is profoundly practical. Our awakening to God leads to drawing away from the temptations of the world to better experience God's light in our daily lives and then to moving through the darkness of our own lives and the world to a union with God and all things. Underhill recognizes that love is at the heart of mysticism, and that our love of God must be joined with our love for the world. Heaven is our destination, but the pathway to heaven is found right here on earth in seeing Christ in yourself and in all others.

My own approach to mysticism affirms the wisdom of both Underhill and Fox. I believe everyday people can have mystical experiences and discern God at the center of their lives and that mystics can be both heavenly minded and earthly good. Mystics can be contemplatives, living lives of prayer and meditation, whose spiritual practices and encounters with God inspire them to become agents of social transformation. Their experiences of divine intimacy enable them to see signs of God's presence everywhere, even in the most unexpected places. Wherever God is hidden, God needs to be unearthed and this often means tearing down the walls of injustice to let God's light shine through.

The mystic in each one of us is unique, just as our personal experiences, vocations, and social location are unique. As I ponder earth-affirming mysticism for our time, I see the mystic adventure as involving the interplay of awakening, affirming, simplifying, expanding, and transforming.

- *Awakening.* Earth-loving mystics awaken to God's grandeur, illuminating all creation. They discover that God's light enlightens every person. All things reveal the presence of God. To expand on Jacob's dream at Beth-el, the house of God, "God was in this place and now I know it." This place is not only where I am, but also in places of sorrow and pain, where God's beloved children are forgotten, marginalized, mistreated, and abused, often by those in power.
- *Affirming.* This world in all its tragic beauty matters. God loves the world and following God involves world-affirmation. God loves our cells as well as our souls. God nurtures our spiritual hungers and also wants us to feed the physically hungry. While heaven is our destination, the pathway to heaven begins here in the complexities of politics and personal life. Christ is incarnate right where we are, in the pain of Roman occupation of Bethlehem felt by Jesus's parents and in the hopelessness of ghetto streets and Appalachian hollows felt by parents today. Divine omnipresence challenges us to pay attention and listen to the joys and sorrows of the world as an inspiration to release the holiness imprisoned and disguised by unjust social structures.
- *Simplifying.* Traditionally identified with the path of purgation, simplicity of life prunes away all the clutter that stands between us and God. According to Jesus, God is the vine, and we are the branches. God trims all the dead branches so that God's spiritual energy will flow in and through us to the world. Mystics live simply so that God and not things becomes the source of

their joy and fulfillment. Simplicity of life joins us with those who lack life's basics, and by our simplicity we become good stewards of our economies and ecologies.

- *Expanding.* Luke 2:52 describes Jesus as "increasing in wisdom and stature, and in divine and human favor." Spiritual growth involves expanding our hearts so that our well-being and the well-being of others become joined. Loving our neighbor as ourselves, we see our neighbor's joy as contributing to our own fulfillment. Spiritual stature involves jettisoning the prison of rugged individualism to embrace world loyalty. In the body of Christ, our joys and sorrows are one. We cannot experience the bliss of God's presence while others experience the misery of poverty and oppression.

- *Transforming.* God calls us to become new creations, not conformed to this world, but transformed by the renewing of our minds (Rom 12:2). God calls us beyond unjust social structures to imagine a world in which all persons have the opportunity for abundant life. Mystics see each moment as a healing moment, in their recognition that although the world is healed one person at a time, we must also shape our society so that our institutions promote wholeness and spiritual growth. While mystics often experience personal equanimity amid the storms of life, they also feel a divine restlessness, grounded in their experience of God's aim at Shalom. Head, heart, and hands are joined in the soup kitchen, hospice, polling place, and picket line.

Mystics never stand still, because God never stands still. God moves providentially and provocatively through history, overturning, with Jesus, the tables of injustice and luring us toward God's peaceable realm. The beyond we seek is within this very moment in all its complexity and conflict. God is in this place, and heaven is where we are, waiting for us to open the door of paradise so that all creation may enjoy the bounty of God. There is a mystic in you that urges you to bring the transcendence of heaven to the complexity and conflict of this good earth.

In the chapters ahead, I invite you to integrate contemplation and action as you read stories of mysticism in action, explore the theological and spiritual foundations of world-affirming mysticism, and discover spiritual practices to awaken your own sense of God's presence in your personal, social, and political involvement. My goal is to invite you on a journey of contemplative activism, grounded in the experiences of twelve mystics, each with their own story, told from the perspective of and for the benefit of twenty-first-century persons. I invite you to allow each mystic to speak personally to you as I share in my interpretation of these mystics—what they mean to me, how I understand them as a twenty-first-century North American, and how they inspire my own spiritual practices. It is my prayer that they will awaken the mystic and social activist in you so that in your time and place you will do something beautiful for God and our world.

1

Reverence for Life: *Albert Schweitzer*

Our spiritual experiences change our lives and can change the world. Contemplation and reflection can drive us from the monastery and ivory tower into the realities of human suffering. While our times of prayer and retreat may temporarily draw us away from the world, times of solitude may also enlarge our spirits, making us more sensitive to the struggles others have as well as our complicity in the injustices of the world. Perhaps, no mystic integrated ivory-tower intellect and care for the vulnerable and forgotten as well as Albert Schweitzer (1875–1965). Some might even question his credentials as a mystic, given his commitment to the practical realities of fund-raising and treating the sick in a missionary hospital in Africa. Schweitzer was a "renaissance person" who excelled as a theologian, biblical scholar, organist, organ builder, and physician. One of the most influential biblical scholars of his time, his *Quest of the Historical Jesus* and *Mysticism of Paul the Apostle* are considered classics in New Testament scholarship.

Born in Alsace, the child of a Protestant minister, Schweitzer had from his childhood a questing and sensitive spirit. He annoyed the adults in his family circle by his constant questions related to doctrine and faith. Early on, he glimpsed what later became his vision of "reverence for life" when he refused to go on a youthful hunting expedition. He saw no reason to take life for purely recreational reasons. Intellectually precocious, he received advanced degrees in philosophy, theology, organ, and tropical medicine. But, at thirty, he received the divine call to be Christ's partner in healing the sick at an outpost hospital in Lambaréné in French Equatorial Africa. His New Testament studies led him to embody the faith of Jesus.

Initially, his quest to practice medicine in Africa was rebuffed because his theological orthodoxy was considered suspect by the French missionary society with whom he sought to work. Schweitzer questioned traditional understandings of Jesus, but faithfully lived out the message of the One who said, "Follow me." It became clear to the young scholar that he wanted to be "a simple human being, doing something small in the spirit of Jesus."[1] Schweitzer found that knowing Jesus could only be found in walking the path of Jesus, that is, in faithfully following the Savior's call in our daily lives whether in the classroom or in the mission field. When asked why he left the academic world to treat the sick of central Africa, he responded simply, "Because my master sent me."[2]

Schweitzer's faith can be described in the final words of his classic *The Quest of the Historical Jesus:*

> He comes to us as One unknown, without a name, as of old, by the lakeside, He came to those men who knew Him not. He speaks to us the same words: "Follow thou me!" and sets us to the tasks which He has to fulfill for our time. He commands. And to those who obey Him, whether they be wise or simple, He will reveal himself in the toils, the conflicts, the sufferings which they shall pass

---

1. Albert Schweitzer, "Letter to Music Critic Gustav von Lupke," quoted in *Albert Schweitzer: The Life of a Great Man*, ed. Jean Pierhal (London: Lutterworth, 1956).

2. James Brabazon, "Introduction," in *Albert Schweitzer: Essential Writings* (Maryknoll, NY: Orbis Books, 2005), 19.

through in His fellowship, and, as an ineffable mystery, they shall learn in their own experience Who He is.[3]

Schweitzer discovered that although Jesus could be found in the scholar's study, lecture hall, and concert stage, Jesus's life-transforming call is most fully experienced when we respond to vulnerable persons who bear the mark of suffering. Our vision of reality is transfigured when we find Christ's face in the lost, lonely, and helpless, and when everything we do is an offering to our Savior.

Those who follow Jesus are challenged to become "practical mystics" or "spirit persons," whose encounter with God transforms their lives, opens their hearts, and gives them strong hands to reach out to the vulnerable of our planet. For these practical mystics, the reign or kingdom of God moves from external reality to heart-felt experience in which one seeks "to bring every thought and action under the sway of the kingdom of God."[4]

Schweitzer felt a kinship with the non-human world. As a teenager, he chose not to hunt but to respect innocent, nonhuman life. Many years later, mystical experiences of the unity and beauty of nature led him to formulate the ethical and spiritual vision that inspired his concept of reverence for life. His encounter with Christ led him to abandon the academic world to minister to suffering people in central Africa. Schweitzer straddled several worlds throughout his life—medicine, administration, theology and biblical studies, and music—and was so heavenly minded that he was truly earthly good!

In Schweitzer we find a mystic who could move mountains to relieve suffering humankind. The grace notes of his musical

---

3. Albert Schweitzer, *The Quest of the Historical Jesus* (London: A. & C. Black, 1931), 401.

4. Albert Schweitzer, "The Conception of the Kingdom of God in the Transformation of Eschatology," epilogue to E. N. Mozley, *The Theology of Albert Schweitzer for Christian Inquirers* (London: A. & C. Black, 1950), 107.

mysticism inspired him to see the value and beauty of nonhuman as well as human life and relieve suffering wherever he found it. He heard the voice of Jesus saying, "Follow me," and then went where his Savior sent him.

Following Jesus leads us to experience the world as both mysterious and wonderful and calls us to be agents in global and personal transformation, serving God's creation in its many manifestations. According to Schweitzer:

> Any profound view of the universe is mystic in that it brings men into spiritual relationship with the Infinite. The concept of reverence for life is ethical mysticism. It allows union with the infinite to be realized by ethical action.[5]

REVERENCE FOR LIFE

At the heart of Schweitzer's practical mysticism is the concept of *reverence for life*. Although Schweitzer took the apophatic path of affirming that the mysteries of God's nature are beyond comprehension, he also discovered that within all life flowed a sacred energy, embodied in each creature's will to live. The phrase "reverence for life" emerged from a mystical experience. On the third day of a riverboat journey up an African river, Schweitzer reports that as "we were making our way through a herd of hippopotamuses, there flashed upon my mind, unseen and unsought, the phrase 'reverence for life.'"[6]

Schweitzer's practical mysticism was grounded in experiences of awe and amazement. He shared one such experience in a letter to his beloved spouse, Hélène:

---

5. Albert Schweitzer, *Out of My Life and Thought: An Autobiography* (Baltimore: Johns Hopkins University Press, 1990), 237.

6. Ibid., 155.

Everything is enveloped in a blue, gossamer veil out of which the distant mountain chain shows like a silhouette ... the fragrance of the hay invigorates the air up here. Late butterflies look for fluttering companions; on the bare fields trees appear in harsh outlines, as if they painted the skeletons of bodies that are still filled with lush vitality. But I see everything in its splendor.[7]

Reverence for life emerges from the vision of beauty and the experience of wonder. In the spirit of Aldous Huxley, Schweitzer lived out the affirmation that when the doors of perception are cleansed and opened, everything becomes infinite and filled with value and beauty. Even the tragedies of life whose existence calls us to compassion are part of a larger tapestry of holiness.

Our reverence for life is grounded in our experience of God as the wise and loving mystery flowing through all things. According to Schweitzer,

Our love of God is akin to reverent love. God is infinite life. Thus the most elementary ethical principle, when understood by the heart, means that out of reverence for the unfathomable, infinite and living Reality we call God, we must never consider ourselves strangers toward any human being. Rather, we must bind ourselves to the task of sharing his experiences and try being of help to him.[8]

Reverence for life joins ethics and mysticism. We honor every other life with the same spirit as we do our own. The love we have

---

7. "Letter to Hélène, September 8, 1902," in *Albert Schweitzer— Hélène Bresslau, The Years Prior to Lambaréné, Correspondence 1902– 1912*, trans. Antje Bultmann Lemke (Syracuse, NY: Syracuse University Press, 2000).

8. Albert Schweitzer, *Reverence for Life* (London: SPCK Press, 1966), 113.

for ourselves, as embodiments of the divine mystery and creativity, inspires us to love all creation, both human and nonhuman. A person is ethical only "when life as such is sacred to him—the life of plants and animals—as well as his fellow men and when he devotes himself to all life that is in need of help."[9] One with all creation, we value all life, human and nonhuman, and see ourselves as kin with all.

Solidarity with Suffering

Schweitzer's vision of spirituality and ethics uniting around the theme of reverence of life inspired him to proclaim the solidarity of all who bear the mark of suffering. In describing his childhood, Schweitzer recalls:

> As far back as I can remember I was saddened by the amount of misery I saw in the world around me. . . . One thing that specially saddened me was that the unfortunate animals had to suffer so much pain and misery. The sight of an old limping horse tugged forward by one man while the other kept beating it with a stick to get it to the knacker's yard at Colmar, haunted me for weeks.
>
> It was quite incomprehensible to me—this was before I began going to school—why in my evening prayers I should pray for human beings only. So when my mother had prayed with me and had kissed me good-night, I used to add silently a prayer that I had composed myself for all living creatures. It ran thus: "O heavenly Father, protect and bless all things that have breath; guard them from all evil, and let them sleep in peace."[10]

---

9. Schweitzer, *Out of My Life and Thought*, 157–58.

10. Albert Schweitzer, *Memoirs of Childhood and Youth*, trans. C. T. Campion (London: George Allen & Unwin, 1924), 40.

Wherever there is experience, there is value. Experience and the capacity for suffering, whether in the human or nonhuman realms, are at the heart of the concept of solidarity and reverence and make a moral claim on us. As followers of Jesus, our spirituality opens our hearts to all who suffer. Like Jesus weeping over Jerusalem or seeing God's presence in the birds of the air and the lilies of the field, our faith invites us to see the holiness in both the non-human and the human world. Like the Buddhist image of the Bodhisattva, who defers enlightenment and escape from the world until all creatures find enlightenment, our spirituality inspires us to respond to pain wherever we see it. Mystics must leave their contemplation to get their hands dirty, rescuing the perishing and caring for the dying. We are part of a beloved community in which our destinies are intertwined. The Graceful Interdependence of life, the body of Christ moving beyond the church to the world, sensitizes our spirits so that the suffering of others becomes our own suffering and the healing of others becomes our own healing.

Mystics feel deeply the joys and sorrows of the world. The walls of individualistic isolationism and community protectionism are broken down and only one lively and interdependent reality remains. Individual self-interest recedes before world loyalty. Christ's face shines in all. Christ's cross is revealed in the pain of the world. Christ's resurrection bursts forth unexpectedly when we join our Savior as companions in healing the earth. God calls us to one thing only amid the tasks of our daily lives—to become "a simple human being, doing something small in the spirit of Jesus."[11]

Reflection: Reverence for Life

At the heart of Albert Schweitzer's vision is reverence for life. For Schweitzer, mysticism is essentially practical in nature. Our spiri-

---

11. Schweitzer, "Letter to Music Critic Gustav von Lupke."

tual experiences shape our ethics. Experiencing God in all things inspires us to respect every creature, humans and nonhumans alike. There are no outsiders in God's grace. All things reflect divine wisdom and deserve our ethical and spiritual consideration. Schweitzer's vision of reverence for life reminds us to:

1. *Devote every action to God, making every action a window into experiencing the sacramental nature of life.*
2. *Rejoice in life's diversity, human and nonhuman alike.*
3. *Contemplate the pain and hopelessness of those who suffer, listening for ways we can share in God's healing ministry.*
4. *Be attentive to those who are considered the "least of these" in our community.*

Albert Schweitzer believed that we come to know God's vision for our lives by following the pathway of our Savior. Jesus calls us to follow him in the ordinary tasks of life, performed with the goal of bringing healing to those who bear the mark of suffering. Every act, regardless of how small, can advance the realm of God. In the spirit of Thérèse of Lisieux, we live our spiritual commitments by doing ordinary things with extraordinary love.

Let us constantly ask Jesus, "What would you have me do in this situation? How can I best contribute to the healing of the world?" Then, let us respond to the insights and intuitions we receive to advance God's realm one act at a time.

Give thanks for life's beauty. Let your experiences of reverence and awe inspire you to treat all creation with gratitude, respect, and care. Reverence for life awakens us to the beauty of creation. It also sensitizes us to the pain of creation. We are all inextricably joined in a dynamic fabric of interdependence, as Martin Luther King Jr. asserted. When one rejoices, all rejoice. When one is enriched spiritually, all are enriched spiritually. When one suffers or is treated unjustly, all suffer pain and injustice.

Mysticism has political implications for Schweitzer. It moves us from individual self-interest to world loyalty and from local action to global concern. Out of our sorrow and empathy, we commit ourselves to ease the pain of all who suffer.

What we do on earth matters to God, not only because God has a bias toward beauty and justice, but because God experiences the joy and pain of the world.

Action

During the days ahead, be attentive to those who are considered the "least of these" in our community. Be attentive to their pain and listen to God's guidance in how you can best respond to the vulnerable, lost, and lonely of our world. This may involve volunteering at a soup kitchen, tutoring an at-risk child, collecting shoes and toiletries for refugee families or providing comfort to undocumented immigrants, calling your congressional representative on a political issue that affects the most vulnerable members of our society, or protesting inequality in your community or the nation.

Prayer of Awareness and Transformation

Loving Companion, whose heart beats in all creation and every creature, we thank you for the abundance of all your creation. Awaken me to the joy and pain of the world. Break my heart, give me tears, and help me see that all of us are connected. In Christ's name.

2

Prophetic Resistance:
Dietrich Bonhoeffer

It is likely that Dietrich Bonhoeffer did not see himself as a mystic in the traditional sense of the word. He was an activist, immersed in the scrum of ecclesiastical and national politics, motivated by his personal encounter with Christ, as witnessed to in scripture and the life of the church. His active prayer life inspired him to challenge the authority of both church and state. He saw God's word, revealed in scripture and spiritual inspiration, as our primary guide in the religious journey. Spiritual practices for him were always relational, contextual, and tethered to scripture rather than the soul's individual journey. Scripture was more than mere words to Bonhoeffer; it was the "thin place" where God addresses us as a Living Word of challenge and promise. In living with scripture, we answer the call of the One who affirmed, "Listen! I am standing at the door, knocking; if you hear my voice and open the door, I will come into you and eat with you, and you with me" (Rev 3:20).

For Bonhoeffer, God was a distinct personality, transcendent yet intimate, who makes ethical claims on humanity. Bonhoeffer did not seek to fly from the "alone to the Alone," as the philosophical mystic Plotinus counseled; nor did Bonhoeffer seek the consolation emerging from the divine within, independent of place and time. God addressed humankind in history through Christ,

Spirit, and scripture, making demands and challenging the status quo, whether individually or socially. The God of scripture and sacrament was real to Bonhoeffer and could be found as truly in political resistance as in meditative prayer. Authentic spirituality joins our relationship with God and our relationship with the world. While worship and prayer are essential to the Christian life, the individual Christian and their community of faith fulfill their vocations only if they exist "for others" and involve themselves in the messiness of political involvement, justice seeking, and care for the vulnerable.

If we affirm African American mystic Howard Thurman's definition of mysticism as "the response of the individual to a personal encounter with God within his own soul . . . effecting the inner quality of the life and its outward expression as its manifestation,"[1] then Bonhoeffer is surely a mystic, whose relationship to God called him to do what would be unthinkable to many Christians—enter into a plot to assassinate Adolf Hitler.

Bonhoeffer's faith and mysticism were this-worldly in nature. Faith must be externally expressed in responding to the crises of our time. According to Bonhoeffer, you can't truly love the world unless you love God, and you can't truly love God unless you love the world. Our encounters with the living God immerse us in the complexity of power dynamics and conflict as we seek to be faithful to God's word in our time and place.

Dietrich Bonhoeffer (1906–1945) was born to privilege. His father was a nationally recognized professor of psychiatry and neurosurgery. He and his siblings were raised to be intellectual and scientific leaders. His family was initially shocked when, as a teenager, Bonhoeffer announced that he would be studying theology, and had a yearning to join theological studies with the practice of ministry. A brilliant student, Bonhoeffer anticipated a career in

---

1. Howard Thurman, *The Creative Encounter* (New York: Harper & Row, 1954).

which pulpit, study, and classroom shaped one another. In 1930, his intellectual adventures took him to America, where he studied at Union Theological Seminary and discovered an affinity with African American religion and its understanding of the church as a place of sanctuary and protest. Yet, despite his academic successes and personal privilege, he was troubled by the political and economic situation in his homeland. Economic uncertainty characterized the lives of the middle and lower middle classes, who often blamed foreigners and native-born Jews for their situation. Governmental leaders seemed ineffective in restoring Germany's former glory or stabilizing the economy. In such moments in national history, people often look for political saviors who will make their nation great again, and German people found that savior in Adolf Hitler, who entranced the German people with visions of national greatness: a Third Reich, in which Aryan supremacy would once again be restored, Germany would again become a world leader, and internal economic and political threats would be silenced. Hitler fanned the flames of nation-first ideologies, claiming that Germany would rise again on the global stage; the mythical Eden would be restored and the nation's enemies would pay for the humiliation they inflicted on the Fatherland.

Even church leaders succumbed to Hitler's vision of German restoration. No doubt, some were inspired by their own nationalistic dreams. Others were fearful of facing persecution and losing their status in church and community. Moreover, many clergy and laity were influenced by the Lutheran doctrine of "two kingdoms," which relegated church and state to separate spheres. From the perspective of two kingdoms theology, the church focused on people's souls and individual ethics and represented the spiritual and sacred spheres of life. The state focused on power dynamics, law and order, and national security, and was not subject to the individualistic piety and ethics of the church. The state's realm was the secular, profane, and embodied. One could be a good Christian, faithful and true in personal ethics, while participating in acts of war and suppression as a public citizen. Despite the radical pacifism and egalitarianism of Jesus's message, particularly in the Sermon on the Mount, most German Christians rendered unto Caesar whatever related to society and citizenship, thus bracketing the ethical demands of the gospel from the political sphere.

After a year in America, Bonhoeffer returned to Germany as a pastor-theologian, but soon found himself at odds with the German government and the established church. Things came to a head when the German Church—what became known as the Reich Church—was asked to affirm an "Aryan clause" that expelled persons of Jewish descent from German churches and advocated creating separate congregations for Jewish Christians. Standing on scripture, especially Paul's towering words in the Letter to the Galatians (such as 3:26–29), a group of German Christians protested the racism of the German Church and established an alternative religious movement, the Confessing Church, which in its inception challenged any identification of Christian faith with race, nationality, or citizenship. The affirmation of God's revelation to the Jewish people was at the heart of the Christian witness and must be central to the life of the church, they protested. Out of the Confessing Church movement came one of the great documents of Christian history, the Barmen Declaration, which affirmed the supremacy of Jesus Christ over every aspect of life, including the Christian's involvement in the state, and rejected the attempts of any political leader to co-opt the church as an agent of the state and subservient to its dictates. Written primarily by Swiss theologian Karl Barth, Barmen's affirmation of Christ leads to the negation of the false gods of land and nation:

> Jesus Christ, as he is attested for us in Holy Scripture, is the one Word of God which we have to hear and which we have to trust and obey in life and in death. We reject the false doctrine, as though the church could and would have to acknowledge as a source of its proclamation, apart

from and besides this one Word of God, still other events and powers, figures and truths, as God's revelation.

We reject the false doctrine, as though there were areas of our life in which we would not belong to Jesus Christ, but to other lords—areas in which we would not need justification and sanctification through him . . .

We reject the false doctrine, as though the church were permitted to abandon the form of its message and order to its own pleasure or to changes in prevailing ideological and political convictions . . .

The declaration proclaims the church's freedom in Jesus Christ who is Lord of every area of life. The church obeys him as God's one and only Word who determines its order, ministry, and relation to the state.[2]

Only Jesus Christ can claim our ultimate loyalty. Christ is our leader, not Adolf Hitler. In standing against Hitler and German nationalism, Bonhoeffer and his colleagues in the German Confessing Church found themselves at odds with both church and state.

In 1935, Bonhoeffer was called to be dean of a clandestine Confessing Church seminary in Pomerania. As dean, he sought to ground ministry in practical spirituality. The seminary curriculum included significant time spent in common worship, morning meditation, and reflection on scripture. In a time of crisis, pastoral resolve needs to be grounded on the solid rock of prayer, biblical reflection, and encounter with the living God. Bonhoeffer's ongoing opposition to the German state led to his dismissal from the faculty of the University of Berlin in 1939 and a ban from public preaching.

---

2. *The Barmen Declaration* (City of Wupperthal, Barmen, Germany, 1934). The Barmen declaration is found in many sources, including http://www.westpresa2.org/docs/adulted/Barmen.pdf.

That same year, Bonhoeffer was invited to teach at Union Theological Seminary in New York. The invitation reflected his standing as a theologian and—more importantly, to his friends and theological admirers—his safety. Other German theologians had chosen, and would choose, to become exiles from the despotic reign of Hitler. After only a month, Bonhoeffer chose to return to Germany. His return was a matter of integrity and faith. The theologian who had denounced "cheap grace," forgiveness without sacrifice, recognized that God wanted him to be with his people, even if this meant persecution. Although he worked and prayed for his nation's defeat in the war, Bonhoeffer believed that he could not participate in his nation's postwar healing process if he abandoned his people in a time of crisis.

In the late 1930s, Bonhoeffer became part of the German resistance movement. He was employed as a military intelligence officer, working for the German government, while at the same time gathering and sharing information with foreign agents for the purpose of overthrowing Hitler's regime. Bonhoeffer was arrested in 1943 for conspiracy against the state, including participation in a failed plot to assassinate Hitler. In prison, Bonhoeffer's life was guided by the practices of prayer and scripture along with pastoral care for his fellow prisoners. From behind prison bars, Bonhoeffer reflected on the question: Where can God be found in a "world come of age," an environment in which most people can live without religion? His insightful and challenging reflections eventually were collected in his *Letters and Papers from Prison,* one of the most influential theological documents of the twentieth century.

Bonhoeffer's participation in the resistance was motivated by his recognition that there is only one kingdom, and that Christ is sovereign over both church and state. In Christ, there is no division between sacred and secular, or sacred and profane. All things belong to Christ, and Christ's followers must become active agents not only in restraining evil but in healing the earth. The

church must not only respond to the suffering of vulnerable people, including victims of the state; the church must prevent further
violence toward the marginalized and persecuted. As Eberhard
Bethge, Bonhoeffer's confidant and collector of his writings,
asserted: "The church should not only care for the victims of the
inexorable wheel of state machinery but should throw a wrench
into the spokes of the wheel."[3] In the spirit of Jesus overturning
the tables at the Jerusalem Temple, Bonhoeffer saw resisting Hitler
as a reflection of his belief that God is sovereign over heaven and
earth, and that at times, we must choose less-than-optimal pathways, even the sword, to restrain evil and seek God's realm on
earth.

Bonhoeffer discovered that God is sovereign even over prison
life. Like Paul, many of whose letters were written from prison,
Bonhoeffer wrote theological epistles and embodied in his daily
life the interplay of spirituality and ministry, praying and reading
scripture, providing pastoral care to fellow inmates, and spending
time praying with them as they faced the anxieties of prison life
and the threat of death.

On April 9, 1945, shortly before Germany was defeated, Bonhoeffer was hanged at the Flossenburg Prison, embodying his own
affirmation from the *Cost of Discipleship:* "When Christ calls to a
man, he bids him come and die."[4] His final sermon, preached at
the Flossenburg Prison on the day of his execution, was based on
the scripture "by his stripes we are healed." In prison, Bonhoeffer turned to writing poetry as well as theology. In one of his
best-known poems, "Who am I?" Bonhoeffer ponders the contrast
between his own self-perception and the way others view him, and
concludes:

---

3. Eberhard Bethge, *Bonhoeffer: Exile and Martyr* (New York:
Seabury Press, 1975), 106.

4. Dietrich Bonhoeffer, *The Cost of Discipleship* (New York:
Macmillan, 1972), 99.

Who am I? They mock me, these lonely questions of mine.
Whoever I am, thou knowest, O God, I am thine.[5]

This remembrance of Bonhoeffer in prison, written by an English officer, captures the spirit of one who found God's presence in chaos as well as calm:

Bonhoeffer always seemed to me to spread an atmosphere of happiness and joy over the least incident and profound gratitude for the mere fact that he was alive. . . . He was one of few persons I have met for whom God was real and always near. . . . On Sunday, April 8, 1945, Pastor Bonhoeffer conducted a little service of worship and spoke to us in a way that went to the heart of all of us. He found just the right words to express the spirit of our imprisonment, the thoughts and resolutions it had brought us. He had hardly ended his last prayer when the door opened and two civilians entered. They said, "Professor Bonhoeffer, come with us." That had only one meaning for all prisoners—the gallows. We said good-by to him. He took me aside: "This is the end, but for me it is the beginning of life." The next day he was hanged in Flossenburg.[6]

WORLDLY CHRISTIANITY

Bonhoeffer's encounter with God is profoundly incarnational and this-worldly. As John's Gospel proclaims, "the Word became flesh and lived among us" (John 1:14). Jesus's ministry was both heavenly minded and earthly good. Jesus did not draw people toward heaven but challenged them to embody God's realm "on earth as it is in heaven" (Matt 6:10). The living God can be found

---

5. Ibid., 20.

6. Dietrich Bonhoeffer, *Life Together* (New York: Harper One, 1954), 13.

only in time. As testified to by the Hebraic prophets, the God of scripture is concerned with history, with honesty in business dealings and government, care for the poor, welcome to the stranger, and faithfulness in relationships. Bonhoeffer asserted that "whoever flees the present, flees God's hours; he who flees time flees God."[7] Our experiences of God do not occur somewhere else or to someone else; they occur as we listen to the morning news, respond to the Syrian refugee crisis, and take our grandchildren to school.

The sovereign God is present everywhere and addresses all creation. In contrast to the "two kingdoms" theology that separates the world into sacred and secular spheres, Bonhoeffer asserted that "there are not two worlds, but rather only *the one world of the reality of Christ*, in which God and the reality of the world are one."[8] Accordingly, authentic mysticism is profoundly this-worldly. There is no separate religious sphere. The heavens in all their magnificence declare the glory of God, and God is found in the suffering of those who experience homelessness and addiction, asylum seekers refused entry into the United States, and victims of state-sponsored injustice and terrorism.

Mysticism enlarges our circle of compassion. Mystics are persons whose senses are open to the currents of grace and forgiveness in their own lives and the streams of challenge in their personal and public lives. God's love for the world inspires our own this-worldly affirmations and love for creation. "One who loves God loves him as the Lord of the earth as it is; one who loves the earth loves it as God's earth. One who loves God's kingdom loves it fully as *God's* kingdom, but also fully as God's *kingdom on earth*."[9]

---

7. Dietrich Bonhoeffer, *Barcelona, Berlin, New York: 1928–1931*, ed. Clifford J. Green; trans. Douglas W. Stott; Dietrich Bonhoeffer Works 10 (Minneapolis: Fortress, 2008), 529.

8. Dietrich Bonhoeffer, *Ethics*, ed. Eberhard Bethge; trans. Neville Horton Smith (New York: Macmillan, 1955).

9. Dietrich Bonhoeffer, "Thy Kingdom Come! The Prayer of

Whole Person Spirituality

As spiritually oriented persons, our choice is not *either* God *or* the world, but *for* God *and* the world. The great commandment challenges us to love God, our neighbor, and ourselves, and our neighbor is anyone in need and humankind in all its challenges. Bonhoeffer believed that spirituality relates to the totality of life. There are no God-free zones. All our lives are lived before God and in relationship to God. Christ comes to us in the cries of youth, mourning the violent deaths of classmates in Sandy Hook and Parkland and children separated from their parents at the US borderlands. We recognize Jesus in the voices of women who have been harassed by political and business leaders and in the faces of those who diminish and demean women. We discover God's voice in our own deepest desires and our joy in the beauty of the earth and loving relationships. Authentic spirituality expands our awareness of the joys and sorrows of the world rather than contracts our circles of concern. While we may withdraw from social involvement for times for prayer, meditation, and retreat, our withdrawal is intended to focus and reset our spiritual GPS so that we may be more attentive to our own deepest desires and the needs of the world. Jesus grew in wisdom and stature, and that is our calling, too.

Whole person spirituality rejoices in the beauty of the earth. In the spirit of Jesus, we revel in God's artistry in the birds of the air and the lilies of the field. We find delight in playing with small children. We experience God's love in the love we have for our life partner, in body, mind, and spirit. Whole-person spirituality also awakens us to the pain of others and our complicity in the evils of our time. Meditation sensitizes us to the tragedy and pain of the

---

the Church-Community for God's Kingdom on Earth," in *Berlin: 1932–1933,* ed. Larry Rasmussen; Dietrich Bonhoeffer Works 12 (Minneapolis: Augsburg Fortress, 2009).

world. Prayer opens us to radical amazement and gratitude for the gifts of life and our opportunity to serve others.

Christ chose to be in the world and to suffer for the world. God in Christ did not remain enthroned outside but reconciled the world by becoming an infant in Bethlehem, a political refugee in Egypt, a woodworker in Nazareth, a companion of sinners, and the crucified victim of the powers and principalities. Jesus spent his whole life as a Jew living in an occupied country, subject to the arbitrary oppression of the Roman occupying forces. In embracing Jesus's experiences of divinity in time, we resolve to be God's companions in healing the planet through responding to Christ in the least of these. Our encounters with God deepen our sense of injustice and increase our empathy with the pain of others and inspire us to confront soul-destroying evil in its many relational and political dimensions.

Our citizenship is both heavenly and earthly, but right now, we are on earth! Bonhoeffer's response to German political decision making—and our response to the political decisions of leaders in North America—is connected to our spiritual values. God is present as much in the voting booth as in the sanctuary.

SOLITUDE AND COMMUNITY

A world-affirming faith is grounded in the balance of solitude and community. Our spiritual lives demand quiet prayer and contemplation; they also require the companionship of persons who share our spiritual values. Bonhoeffer expresses this essential polarity in *Life Together,* written as a primer for seminarians but equally helpful to lay persons:

> *Let him who can't be alone beware of community.* He will only do harm to himself and the community. Alone you stood before God when he called you; alone you had to answer that call; alone you had to struggle and pray; and

alone you will die and give account to God. . . . If you refuse to be alone you are refusing God's call to you, and can have no part in the community of those who are called. . . . *Let him who is not in community beware of being alone.* Into the community you were called; it was not meant for you alone; in the community of the called you bear your cross, you struggle, you pray. You are not alone, even in death, and on the Last Day you will be only one member of the congregation of Jesus Christ.[10]

Jesus went to a secluded place to pray, after a hard day's work of preaching, teaching, and healing (Mark 1:21–39). From his time of seclusion, Jesus strengthened his resolve to share the good news throughout Judea. Later, in his own time of trial, Jesus retreated to the Garden of Gethsemane to pray for guidance and strength for the suffering to come. In silence and solitude, Jesus realigned his will with God's will to find greater calm and courage to face arrest, humiliation, and the cross (Mark 14:32–42). We need to claim our own times of solitude so that we might bear our own crosses of service and sacrifice with grace, compassion, and forgiveness.

Bonhoeffer believed that our times of solitude propel us into action, enhance our sense of purpose and empathy with others' pain, and guide our political involvements. In silence and solitude, we gain perspective that enables us to persevere despite opposition and conflict and find calm in times of stress. Our involvement in community enables us to live out the graceful moments we experience in solitude by becoming Christ's presence to persons in need and Christ's challenge to unjust social structures. Spirituality takes shape in relationships, especially with those living in adverse circumstances. Grounded in a largeness of soul, persons of spirit embrace life in its many dimensions rather than flee life's

---

10. Bonhoeffer, *Life Together,* 77.

complexities. Written as air-raid sirens blared throughout the concentration camp, Bonhoeffer affirmed the solidarity of life:

> Christianity puts us into many dimensions of life at the same time; we make room for ourselves, to some extent for God, and for the whole world. We rejoice with those who rejoice, we weep with those who weep; we are anxious (—I was again interrupted just then by the alert, and now sitting outdoors enjoying the sun—) about our lives, but at the same time, we must think about things more important than life itself. When the alert goes, for instance: as soon as we turn our minds away from worrying about our own safety to the task of helping other people keep calm, the situation is completely changed; life isn't pushed back into a single dimension, but is kept multi-dimensional and polyphonous.[11]

Spiritual practices and faith in the living God of history take us, as Bonhoeffer reveals, from individual fear to relational courage and enable us to grow in stature so that our well-being and the well-being of others is one.

The Living Word in a World Come of Age

In many ways, Bonhoeffer was prophetic of twenty-first-century religion in his understanding of a world come of age that no longer needed the theological doctrines, articles of faith, external religious authorities, or the existence of God to navigate the challenges of life. Anticipating our twenty-first-century pluralistic and postmodern world and foreshadowing our own contemporary political challenges in his opposition to the actions of the German state, which used religion for its own purposes, Bonhoeffer

---

11. Dietrich Bonhoeffer, *Letters and Papers from Prison* (New York: Macmillan, 1972), 310–11.

recognized that spiritual and theological systems that focused on guilt, obedience to authority figures, censorship of diverse opinions, or human sin and weakness, no longer addressed people in the modern world. Bonhoeffer queried, "What is Christianity for us today?" We ask the same question, "What is spirituality for us today in a time of a plethora of spiritual options, hybrid spiritualities that join the practices and beliefs of many traditions, self-help and prosperity spiritualities, and a reliance on personal experience rather than ecclesiastical or doctrinal authority?" With Bonhoeffer, we ponder how we may best share the Christian message and Christian spiritual practices with people who can do without God in their daily lives and find the traditional practices of worship and spiritual discipline irrelevant to their daily lives. How do we invite persons who spend Sunday mornings at Starbucks or at sporting events with their children to explore their own spiritual yearnings?

Bonhoeffer is clear that every person has spiritual inclinations that must not be diminished or looked down upon by those who have explicit commitments to spiritual practices, communal worship, or theological reflection. There is a Godward movement in every life, despite the fact that it is often crowded out by the cares, duties, and obligations of contemporary times. Spiritual leaders must address persons in terms of their strengths, not their weaknesses. Spiritual growth is not the result of shaming or creating guilt where none is felt but in addressing people in their current spiritual, economic, and relational condition, with affirmation rather than judgment. We must speak of God in a nonreligious way, listening to the joy and pain within ourselves and in those who no longer believe they need the comforts and consolations of religion. "The world that has come of age is more godless, and perhaps for that reason, nearer to God, than the world before its coming to age."[12] Christ addresses us right where we are in the challenges and possibilities of our lives. We can

---

12. Ibid., 362.

find God amid the clatter of pots and pans in the kitchen. We can experience God's love on the teeming streets of Calcutta, with Mother Teresa, as we do something beautiful for God. We can feel as if our legs are praying, with Abraham Joshua Heschel and Martin Luther King Jr., as we protest unjust laws. We can experience the heartbeat of God as we attend a March for Our Lives and hear God's voice speaking through young persons, calling for safety in their schools and the city streets. We can find God in protesting against tyrants and serving time in prison for our willingness to undermine despots who substitute loyalty to them for loyalty to God.

A spirituality for a world come of age is relational and sacrificial. Every Christian is called to be a person for others. The church is called to be a church for the world, most particularly for those beyond the church whose suffering touches God's own heart. Spirituality expands our circle of compassion and challenges us to address pain wherever we find it, whether in personal relationships or public policy. In Bonhoeffer's case, his sense of God's call to be a person for others led to him praying for the defeat of his nation and entering the resistance movement to prevent further suffering and destruction. God's way is larger than our own well-being, the survival of our churches, and the success of our nation.

Only a Suffering God Can Save

Dietrich Bonhoeffer believed that God is involved in every encounter. God is concerned about our personal lives and political decision making. Although God is sovereign, God is also relational and immanent. God's power is present in God's empathy with humankind. Bonhoeffer's vision is profoundly biblical in spirit, following Paul's description of the incarnation in Philippians 2:

> Let the same mind be in you that was in Christ Jesus,
> who, though he was in the form of God,

did not regard equality with God
as something to be exploited,
but emptied himself,
taking the form of a slave,
being born in human likeness.
And being found in human form,
he humbled himself
and became obedient to the point of death—
even death on a cross. (Phil 2:5–11)

Bonhoeffer recognized that our understanding of God's nature shapes our spiritual practices and ethical and political actions. The distant, dominating God of much of popular religion who rules by edict and demands absolute obedience inspires dominating, coercive, and dictatorial behaviors. A deity who separates the sheep and the goats and the righteous and unrighteous leads to behaviors of exclusion and persecution of those who differ from us. A god who divides the world in terms of sacred and secular leads to the creation of exclusively secular spheres, outside the realm of faith and ethics and unrelated to the message of Jesus. The flames of the Holocaust burn brightly when we see God as on our side and others as outside God's care. In contrast, Bonhoeffer saw God's identity most fully revealed in the cross, God's willingness to sacrifice and suffer for our salvation and God's identification with our pain and suffering as God's own distress. According to Bonhoeffer, "the Bible directs man to God's powerlessness and suffering; only the suffering God can help."[13]

In our time in which spirituality is often identified with prosperity, good fortune, equanimity, and success, and religious leaders have compromised their integrity for political gain, Bonhoeffer sees the joy of discipleship as connected with our ability

---

13. Ibid., 361.

to empathize with God's pain in the pain of those around us. Large-hearted spirituality grieves with those who suffer, protests with those seeking justice, and rejoices with those who experience healing and restoration.

Reflection: Prophetic Resistance

Dietrich Bonhoeffer saw spirituality as involving the whole person in her or his historical setting. Our encounter with God inspires us to be God's companions in social and political transformation. God's vision of Shalom calls us to embodied, creation-centered spirituality. Spiritual practices turn us toward history and politics, even when done in solitude. Our commitment to prayer, scripture, and meditation sensitizes us to the pain of the world and inspires us to actions to prevent suffering for our contemporaries and future generations. There are many ways to practice prophetic resistance. It may involve calling your political representatives, participating in a protest or march, becoming active in local or national politics, or challenging governmental policies through acts of nonviolent resistance. What is important is that we find creative ways to embody our faith in daily life as individuals and citizens who seek God's realm on earth as it is in heaven. Bonhoeffer invites us to embodied spirituality in the following practices:

1. *Pray without ceasing, asking God to open your heart to the world's suffering.*
2. *Read the scriptures and other sacred literature prayerfully, listening for their meaning in our current social context.*
3. *Give thanks for the opportunity to put your prayers in action, reaching out to the vulnerable and challenging the forces of injustice.*
4. *Listen to the news prayerfully, noting situations that call you to political involvement.*

Dietrich Bonhoeffer believed that God comes to us in the public as well as private spheres of life. There is only one kingdom, God's world, and Christians are called to be full participants in the political sphere. Bonhoeffer saw the evil of his nation's leaders and the damage they were doing to the church and heard God's call to prevent the occurrence of future evils. An older contemporary of Bonhoeffer's, Harry Emerson Fosdick, penned words appropriate to Bonhoeffer's situation as well as our own in the twenty-first century:

> Save us from weak resignation
> to the evils we deplore;
> let the gift of your salvation
> be our glory evermore.
> Grant us wisdom, grant us courage,
> serving you whom we adore,
> serving you whom we adore.[14]

Action

The earth in its entirety belongs to God. God calls us to be healers and stewards, promoting well-being for all creation and challenging us to be God's companions in seeking Shalom. As daunting as this task is, it begins with prayerful mindfulness of our world. What evils do you notice? Where are persons and institutions choosing death rather than life? Where is injustice being perpetrated by our own nation? Recognizing that none of us can claim to be innocent bystanders in our digital world, what evil do you feel prayerfully called to confront?

In the course of writing this book, I participated in a "March for Our Lives" event near my home on Cape Cod. My wife and I

---

14. Harry Emerson Fosdick, "God of Grace and God of Glory" (1930).

contacted our representatives, urging them to promote gun safety and regulation of firearms. In our own "Bonhoeffer moment," my wife and I have also alerted our representatives to support refugee resettlement in Massachusetts and across the nation and called the White House to encourage the president to reconsider his decision to pull out of the Paris Climate Accords. We have protested through vigils and phone calls the separation of children and their parents on the US border. These are small actions, reflecting our spiritual commitments, but they can become a tipping point in supporting the moral arc of the universe when we join with others.

What is your "Bonhoeffer moment"? In the intricate interdependence of life, we all have skin in the game. What current crisis calls you to prayer and appropriate social and political involvement? Spiritual practices challenge us to love the earth as well as heaven!

Prayer of Awareness and Transformation

In this moment of time, help me find my calling as your companion in healing the world. Let my voice ring out for peace, justice, and earth care. Let my prayers move me to action, and may I become an agent of healing for this good earth. In Christ's name. Amen.

3

Empathetic Spirituality: Simone Weil

Mystical experiences can occur both inside and outside religious institutions. Mysticism often leads spiritual seekers beyond the orthodox boundaries of faith to embrace God's presence outside the church. Mystical experiences can also inspire seekers to question institutional authority and theological orthodoxy, when religious bodies become instruments of exclusion, denying divine revelation in the sciences, philosophy, and other faiths. The affirmation "wherever there is truth, God is its source" may lead mystics to challenge church doctrines that threaten the quest for truth in science, medicine, economics, and personal experience. Simone Weil exemplified the "outsider" saint, who refused to be baptized as a Roman Catholic as a witness to her quest for intellectual truth and in solidarity with all who were outside the church. While she honored the Roman Catholic tradition, she could not in good conscience check her mind at the door of the church, nor could she give allegiance to a faith that placed the future of unbaptized infants in limbo. She clearly asserted that she would not enter the Roman Catholic Church unless God clearly demanded it. Weil's empathetic mysticism was reflected in a permeable spirituality in which the pain of others was her pain and the struggles of others, especially the humiliated and dispossessed, were her struggles.

Simone Weil was born to an upper-middle-class French family on February 3, 1909. The child of nominally religious Jewish parents, Simone's father was a highly regarded physician; her mother, a consummate caregiver; and her brother was to become a world-renowned mathematician. As a child, Simone was both intellectually precocious and extraordinarily empathetic. At age five, she chose not to eat sugar in solidarity with the French troops fighting on her nation's behalf. She was a brilliant student, who attended France's most prestigious educational institutions, excelled in philosophy, and embarked on a teaching career in her early twenties. Throughout her life, Simone's health was fragile, reflected in constant migraine headaches, beginning at age fourteen and lasting the remainder of her short life.

The Celtic spiritual tradition speaks of "thin places," which are transparent to the divine in their unity of heaven and earth. Certain persons may be described as "thin persons," that is, individuals whose selves embrace the pain of others as if it were their own. The humiliation of others becomes their humiliation, and the joy of others becomes their joy. Surely, this is what the apostle Paul means when he describes the intricate interdependence of the body of Christ: "If one member suffers, all suffer together with it; if one member is honored, all rejoice together with it" (1 Cor 12:26).

In her early twenties, Simone identified with the French workers' movement. In the wake of the Russian revolution, workers throughout Europe demanded better working conditions, greater self-determination, and living wages. While Simone, like most French intellectuals of her time, explored Marxism, her concern for workers' well-being was empathetic rather than ideological. She felt a unity of spirit with the humiliated proletariat that at times caused her to be critical of communist party policies and power politics, when they placed—as did the church—ideology above human welfare, including the workers whose well-being they sought.

In 1935–1936, Simone took a leave of absence from teaching to work in a French factory. Despite her ill health, she needed to experience firsthand the soul-numbing work and personal humiliation workers daily experienced. She discovered that factory workers' daily humiliation led to a loss of personal dignity that caused workers to abandon any sense of agency and self-esteem in the quest for their own survival and that of their family. Their spirits were stunted and robbed of experiences of beauty, which lead us to the divine beauty beyond time and space. Simone recognized that unlike the factory workers with whom she was joined at the workplace and who received meager wages, she was a person of privilege who could return to her teaching post and receive financial support from her parents should she need it. Several years later, Simone worked on a farm in order to experience the real lives of farm workers.

Weil traveled to Spain during the Spanish Civil War to support the leftist movement's quest for freedom and self-determination and was injured when she stepped in a pot of cooking oil. This accident likely saved her life; the battalion with which she had been associated was annihilated in battle.

With the beginning of World War II, Simone supported the French resistance to Nazi occupying forces, and sought, perhaps unrealistically in terms of her health, to be sent behind enemy lines to aid her nation in a clandestine role. During her time in England, working for the French government in exile, she contracted tuberculosis. She refused the rich diet required to support her recovery to maintain solidarity with her compatriots in occupied France. Empathetic with their distress, even in ill health, she did not want to have comforts that others lacked. She died, virtually unknown, on August 23, 1943, at age thirty-four. Weil might have died in anonymity except for the fact that her journals and letters were circulated posthumously by those who saw the holiness of her spirit and the wisdom of her writings. Readers saw her as a saint for the modern age, deeply spiritual yet connected with the daily life of the poor. Her erudite and challenging writing was not merely ivory-tower peroration, unrelated to the complexities of daily life, but reflected her identification with the poor, her discovery of God in the pain and beauty of life, and her faithful iconoclasm in relationship to the church she loved. It is unclear whether Simone Weil was baptized during her final days. She trusted that God would compel her to become officially part of the Roman Catholic Church if it was the divine will. She prized the quest for truth and integrity above institutional orthodoxy.

While Simone Weil claimed that she did not seek dramatic experiences of God and was suspicious of most forms of prayer, her life, in the spirit of the title of one of her best-known collections of writings, could be described as "waiting for God." Her unsought mystical experiences demonstrated to Weil the reality of a God who seeks us out and pursues us until we find ourselves in God's loving presence. Weil's life was transformed by a series of unexpected mystical experiences occurring in her mid-twenties, which she describes in letters written to a Roman Catholic priest, Father Perrin, her confidant and spiritual advisor.

The first of her self-reported mystical experiences occurred following her arduous year as a factory worker. In order to recuperate from the demands of factory work on her fragile health, her parents took her on holiday to Portugal. Weil traveled to a Portuguese fishing village, where she observed the festival of its patron saint. In her words:

> I was alone and it was a full moon over the sea. The wives
> of the fisherman were, in procession, making a tour of all
> the ships, carrying candles and singing what must cer-
> tainly be ancient hymns of heart-wrenching sadness. . . .
> There the conviction was suddenly borne in upon me that
> Christianity was pre-eminently a religion of slaves, that
> slaves can't help belonging to it, and I among others.[1]

---

1. Simone Weil, *Waiting for God* (New York: Harper Collins, 2009), 26.

While Weil does not clearly define the nature of spiritual slavery in her autobiographical writings, I believe it applies to our utter dependence on God, when all else fails, as the source of healing, redemption, and sustenance in time of need. When we are weakest, we discover with the apostle Paul's affirmation following his own mystical experience of divine care that God's "grace is sufficient for you, for power is made perfect in weakness. So, I will boast all the more gladly of my weaknesses, so that the power of Christ may dwell in me" (2 Cor 12:9). When we discover our nothingness, fallibility, and weakness, God becomes everything to us, and with our ego set aside, we begin to see the world through the eyes of God, who sees our world through us. Perhaps, like the apostle Paul, who referred to himself as a prisoner for Christ, Weil saw true spiritual freedom as openness and surrender to God's will moving through us. In the spirit of the apostle, she sought a type of spiritual perfection in which we become a living Eucharist: "we no longer live in ourselves but Christ lives in us," as our guiding, animating, and controlling spirit.[2]

The second experience Weil reports occurred in 1937, during a time of recuperation at Assisi, Italy, when "something stronger than me compelled me for the first time in my life to go down on my knees."[3] A year later, during a severe migraine attack, occurring in Holy Week, Weil felt deep within her the passion of Christ, a feeling that continued throughout her life. She experienced what the apostle Paul describes as the divine kenosis, letting go of power and transcendence to save humankind.

Weil discovered that literature and scripture can transform one's life. Over the next several years, whenever she recited the Lord's prayer in Greek, she experienced the ecstasy of divine presence, which took her beyond space and time, relieved her pain, and was realized through surrendering her will to God's will regardless of the circumstances of life. Weil discovered the transforming power

---

2. Ibid., 36.
3. Ibid., 26.

of poetry while reciting George Herbert's poem "Love," which had
been recommended by an English priest.

> Love bade me welcome, yet my soul drew back,
>> Guilty of dust and sin.
> But quick-ey'd Love, observing me grow slack
>> From my first entrance in,
> Drew nearer to me, sweetly questioning
>> If I lack'd anything.
> "A guest," I answer'd, "worthy to be here";
>> Love said, "You shall be he."
> "I, the unkind, the ungrateful? Ah my dear,
>> I cannot look on thee."
> Love took my hand and smiling did reply,
>> "Who made the eyes but I?"
> "Truth, Lord, but I have marr'd them; let my shame
>> Go where it doth deserve."
> "And know you not," says Love, "who bore the blame?"
>> "My dear, then I will serve."
> "You must sit down," says Love, "and taste my meat."
>> So I did sit and eat.

Throughout her life, the poem was a source of healing and consolation, especially when migraines threatened to overwhelm her.

> Often, at the culminating point of a violent headache, I
> make myself say it over, concentrating all my attention
> upon it and clinging with all my soul to the tenderness
> it enshrines. I used to think I was merely reciting it as a
> beautiful poem, but without my knowing it, the recita-
> tion had the virtue of a prayer. It was during one of these
> recitations that, as I told you, Christ himself came down
> and took possession of me.[4]

---

4. Ibid., 27.

Weil's reflections and mystical experiences led her to a sacramental vision of her life and the world, which universalized the spirit of the Roman Catholic Mass. Weil believed that our true dignity and vocation occurs when "we no longer live in ourselves, but Christ lives in us; so that through our perfection Christ, in his integrity and indivisible unity, becomes in a sense each one of us, as he is completely in each host."[5]

In her openness to God moving through the events of our lives and calling us toward solidarity with others, Weil exemplifies her own philosophy of sainthood. She perceived her times as unprecedented, with the rise of the workers' movement, political revolutions, and constant rumors of war. Our times are unprecedented as well, with rising pluralism, mistrust of institutions, including the church, polarization in the body politic, nuclear saber rattling, xenophobia, and global climate change. We, too, are challenged to be saints for our time.

> Today it is not merely enough to be a saint, but we must have the saintliness demanded by the present moment, a new saintliness without precedent. . . . A new type of sanctity is indeed a fresh spring, an invention. If all is kept in proportion and if the order of each thing is preserved, it is almost equivalent to a new revelation of the universe and of human destiny. It is the exposure of a large portion of truth and beauty hitherto concealed under a thick layer of dust.[6]

Weil's life and work challenges us: you can be a mystic, you can be a saint, you can surrender to grace and let God work in and through your life to change the world.

---

5. Ibid., 36.
6. Ibid., 51.

Mysticism as Waiting on God

Weil believed that God comes to us through our experience as finite and dependent creatures. God creates by withdrawing God's power from the world, so that creation might have its own freedom and integrity. Yet, although God's withdrawal may lead to experiences of divine absence, the divine withdrawal allows us to come to the One whose presence energizes the world order in its totality. Jesus saves us, as Philippians 2:5–11 asserts, by humbling himself, becoming like a slave. By following the path of Jesus, and bending to God's will, we can experience God's presence in times of affliction as well as in visions of beauty. Slavery, as Weil understands it, involves the denial of the brittle and self-interested ego to make room for God of the universe to occupy and transform our selves. God becomes most real to us when we allow God to become God for us and not an object reflecting our own self-interest and biases. In surrendering our freedom and individuality to God's higher vision, we become God's instruments of healing and transformation in our world.

Affliction and Beauty as Windows into Divinity

God addresses us through the order of the universe in all its wondrous complexity and tragic beauty. All things, Weil asserts, are intermediaries between God and us and can for those who pay attention awaken us to divinity in a world that both hides and reveals divinity. God comes to us primarily in times of affliction, when we recognize our total dependence on forces beyond our power. Affliction emerges in life's most challenging moments, when we experience suffering, humiliation, and loss of social standing. Such moments can occur as a result of illness; they can also occur through injustice and poverty, when persons in power fail to recognize our humanity. Affliction can destroy or ennoble our spiritual lives, depending on our approach to it. Few people wish to experience a debilitating illness, but illness can drive us to our knees and awaken our need for God and other persons. Hitting what we perceive to be rock bottom, in illness or addiction we can become inspired to trust ourselves to a power greater than ourselves. We discover the meaning of Charlotte Elliott's hymn, "Just as I Am," popularized in the altar calls at Billy Graham Crusades:

> Just as I am, tho' tossed about,
> With many a conflict, many a doubt,
> Fightings within and fears without,
> O Lamb of God, I come, I come!
> Just as I am, poor, wretched, blind,
> Sight, riches, healing of the mind,
> Yea, all I need in Thee to find,
> O Lamb of God, I come, I come!

Weil recognizes that affliction is ambiguous; it can destroy the spirit as well as awaken us to the freedom found in letting God guide us through the valley of the shadow. In accepting our dependence on God and others, we are freed from the prison of rugged individualism and isolated independence. In embracing our vulnerability, we open to the fullness of God's mercy. We become slaves, obeying a power and wisdom greater than our own. As another hymn, "Rock of Ages," asserts, "Nothing of my own I bring, simply to the cross I cling." Affliction breaks down every screen we place between God and ourselves. If we pay attention to the grace within the worst of times, we may discover that fully relying on God opens the door to the best of times. I have found this to be the case in those times when I admitted my own brokenness and abandoned all attempts at self-reliance and threw myself solely upon God's grace. More than a few of my congregants have confessed that when they opened to their powerlessness, asking for God's help and the help of God's human messengers, their prayers were answered. In our weakness, God's strength heals us. This is not passivity, but trust in God that empowers us to work out our salvation in fear and trembling, knowing that everything comes through grace.

God ministers to us in pain; God transforms us in ecstasy. Affliction and beauty are at the heart of God's good creation. Within each person is an inclination toward beauty. "A sense of beauty, although mutilated, distorted, and soiled, remains rooted in the heart of man as a powerful incentive. It is present in the preoccupations of secular life."[7] God comes to us in experiences of beauty as well as love. "Just as God hastens into every soul and immediately it opens, even a little, in order for it to love and serve the afflicted, so he descends in all haste to love and admire the tangible beauty of his own creation through the soul that opens to him."[8] Our love of beauty is essentially "longing for the Incarnation."[9] In the spirit of the philosopher Plato, whose vision inspired Weil's understanding of the universe, Weil asserts that "beauty is eternity here below."[10]

ACCEPTING THE WHOLE OF LIFE AS DIVINE REVELATION

The world we typically experience is an ambiguous revelation of the divine. In the spirit of Jewish mysticism and Paul's doctrine of kenosis in Philippians, Weil believes that God withdraws from the world in order to give the world existence of its own. In the divine withdrawal, God gives up power and risks the crucifixion of Jesus as well as the crucifixions experienced daily by God's afflicted creatures. Yet, the hidden and apparently distant God remains the energy and wisdom moving through all things.

---

7. Ibid., 103.
8. Ibid.
9. Ibid., 109.
10. Ibid., 110.

God's ordering of the universe sustains and heals, but it also can bring pain and sorrow. The interplay of "gravity" and "grace" is essential to Weil's vision of the universe. We absolutely depend on the divinely created and sustained order of the universe to go about our daily lives and plan for the future. Gravity keeps my feet on the ground as I rejoice in my sunrise walk on Cape Cod's Craigville, Covell's, and Dowses beaches. Gravity's dependability enables me to sit in my writing chair and compose these words as well as to make a jump shot in a basketball game with my grandson. Yet, the force of gravity can also bring me pain. A fall to the ground can disable me; a falling rock can send me to the emergency room. The waves that inspire can also wash away seaside homes; the dependable warmth of the sun is a factor in skin cancer and will eventually incinerate our planet. Within gravity, the necessities of life, often revealed in apparent mindless and purposeless chance, there is the grace of divine incarnation not only in the birth, ministry, death, and resurrection of God's Son Jesus, but in the hints of beauty that draw us heavenward and the moments of divine inspiration that come unbidden solely as a gift of God. In order to embrace the wonder of life, we must also accept life's brevity and pain. Though oft hidden from our eyes, all things are intermediaries revealing indirectly and partially God's presence. When we "pay attention," as Weil describes the essence of prayer, we can experience all creation as flowing from a wise and generous hand and affirm that whether we live or die, we are God's beloved.

The affirmation of the universe in its totality enables us to proclaim with the afflicted Job, "though he kill me, I will trust in him" (Job 13:15). The most righteous of humans, the legendary Job, loses everything—property, children, social standing, respect, and health—and while he does not receive an explanation for the evils he experiences, God gives him a vision of the incredibly wild and amazing universe that fills him with awe and wonder.

The wise energy of creation, often apparently withdrawn from our senses and experiences, speaks to us through all things. These intermediaries are "go-betweens" between God and the world, bridges "by which love passes from God to us and us back to God. It is something by which God is indirectly present in the world," whether in terms of "beautiful physical objects," the harmony of the spheres, human creativity, social relations, or "even our own inner states."[11] According to one commentator, "when we pay attention to the beauty that the entire world presents to us, we allow it to reveal the deep purpose that binds the whole creation together."[12] In paying attention and affirming the world in all its tragic beauty, we draw near to God and begin to see ourselves and the world through God's eyes.

In surrendering to God, we begin to see the world with God's vision, and God sees the world through our experience. Surrender to God in all things doesn't lead to acquiescing to the unjust status quo. The affliction of workers, undocumented immigrants, refugees, victims of the traumas of racism and sexism, and the pain of persons who experience abuse are not God's will, despite God's presence as the energy and order of the universe that gives life to both oppressor and oppressed. God feels this pain as well and wants us to respond. God's incarnational love is aimed at inspiring greater love and beauty, enabling people to experience God more fully in the order of the universe and the beauty it reveals. Small acts of kindness and willingness to sacrifice for causes greater than us can change the world. When God calls us to empathetic justice, then, as the Hebraic prophets discovered, our anger is God's anger, our protest is God's protest, our justice-seeking is God's justice-seeking, and our love is God's love. In moments of transparency, we let God see through us and act through us, accepting our role as agents of social transformation. Seen from this per-

---

11. Eric O. Springsted, *Simone Weil and the Suffering of Love* (Eugene, OR: Wipf & Stock, 2010), 104.

12. Ibid.

spective, another of the revival hymns from my childhood, written during a time of the writer's personal distress, takes on new meaning as the way of Jesus becomes the way of social healing and Shalom-seeking:

> Have Thine own way, Lord!
> Have Thine own way!
> Thou art the potter I am the clay.
> Mold me and make me after Thy will,
> While I am waiting, yielded and still.
> Have Thine own way, Lord!
> Have Thine own way!
> Search me and try me, Master, today!
> Whiter than snow, Lord, wash me just now,
> As in Thy presence humbly I bow.
> Have Thine own way, Lord!
> Have Thine own way!
> Hold over my being absolute sway!
> Filled with Thy spirit till all can see
> Christ only, always, living in me.[13]

When we experience Christ living in us, our obedience to a power and love greater than our own awakens us to authentic freedom, trust in God's grace, and identification with suffering persons as God's beloved, inspiring us to greater love.

Reflection: Empathetic Spirituality

Simone Weil experienced God in the affliction and humiliation of the poor and dispossessed and in her own personal debilitation. She discovered that the boundaries between herself and the pain of the world were porous. She experienced Christ in

---

13. Adelaide A. Parker, "Have Thine Own Way."

identifying with the "least of these." Those who are experiencing homelessness, poverty, and injustice are our spiritual companions. Their pain is our pain and their joy our celebration. Our own identification with the marginalized breaks down the walls of giver and receiver, helper and helped, insider and outsider. With the apostle Paul, we can experience the reality that beneath our social and economic distinctions, "there is no longer Jew or Greek, there is no longer slave or free, there is no longer male and female; for all of you are one in Christ Jesus" (Gal 3:28). Following Simone Weil,

1. *Let God speak to you in poetry and literature, such as George Herbert's poem "Love," Maya Angelou's "On the Pulse of the Morning," Mary Oliver's "The Summer Day," or Gerard Manley Hopkins's "God's Grandeur."*
2. *Meditatively pray the Lord's Prayer, asking God's guidance in sharing in Jesus's vision of God's realm "on earth as it is in heaven."*
3. *Pay attention to God's presence in your pain and the pain of others.*
4. *Immerse your senses in beauty. Look for beauty everywhere and make a commitment to add to the beauty of the world in every action.*

Simone Weil saw both affliction and beauty as pathways to experiencing God. God comes to us in the joyful and painful and often is disguised in difficult situations and challenging people.

Simone Weil saw beauty hidden in unlikely persons and places. Have you ever seen a geode? If not, look up a photo on the internet. At first glance, the geode is nondescript, usually rough-hewn, and not necessarily appealing. But break open a geode, and behold you will find something uniquely beautiful within. The same geodic reality is found within the lives of the afflicted and humiliated, and in our own moments of affliction and humiliation. But we need to pay attention, to see the beauty within the nondescript, ugly, discarded, and painful realities of life. In paying attention, God comes alive to us in our joys and sorrows, and we experience God's providence providing guidance in our personal and political involvements.

Action

Simone Weil recognizes that when we reflect on our experiences and pay attention to others, something of beauty may emerge in our interactions. Recently, in embracing my grief at another school shooting, I was moved to hold a prayer service at our church and to take the first steps in responding to gun violence, personally and politically. Simone Weil knew that moments of pain and debilitation invite us to go from independence to interdependence, to ask for help and then receive the graces of those around you. Toward what social justice issue is God calling you? Whom do you need to call upon to be your partner or partners in responding to the injustices in your community and nation?

Prayer of Awareness and Transformation

God, keep me awake today. Open my heart to all creation, sensing your presence in joy and sorrow. Let me walk in beauty today and in every encounter seek to bring beauty into the world and lighten the spirits of those around me. In Christ's name. Amen.

4

Head, Heart, and Hands:
Rufus Jones

Philosopher and spiritual guide Kerry Walters describes Rufus
Jones (1863–1948) as a "mystic of the everyday."[1] In the spirit
of his Quaker heritage, Jones believed that the divine light illuminated everything and that ordinary events and everyday people
are chock-full of divinity. Although Jones affirmed the mystery of
divine existence and recognized that no words can fully describe
the Holy One, he described his own and the Quaker approach to
spirituality as an "affirmative mysticism," grounded in the recognition that finite humans can directly experience and respond to
ultimate reality. As Kerry Walters notes, "This only makes sense,
given Jones's conviction that the universe shimmers with the presence of the incarnate God and that the human spirit is essentially
conjunct with Spirit."[2] We don't have to flee the world to find God.
God is as near as our next breath, and divine light illumines every
encounter, making each moment a portal into divinity. Mysticism
is not the obliteration of the self but the fulfillment and expansion
of our selves to be in sync with the Divine Self. As the philosopher
Alfred North Whitehead averred, peace is not anesthesia but the

---

1. Kerry Walters, ed., *Rufus Jones: Essential Writings* (Maryknoll,
NY: Orbis Books, 2001), 15.
2. Ibid., 30.

broadening and deepening of self in such a way that my individual self-interest is joined with the well-being of all creation.

Deep down, we are all mystics in the making. We just don't realize it. Mysticism is an awakening to our deepest reality, the inner light of God that illumines our spirits and gives life and light to the world.

We are part of a vast ocean of experience. Though uniquely centered in our vantage point on the universe, we are also like waves in an infinite sea of divinity. As Jones notes:

> We do not know how far the margins of our own being reach. We cannot completely map the full area that belongs to us. No one can with certainty map the boundary between himself and the beyond himself, any more than we can tell where the tidal river ends and the ocean begins, but we unmistakably feel on occasions that tides from beyond our own margins sweep into us and refresh us.[3]

Born in a devout and devoted Quaker household, Rufus Jones lived and breathed the Quaker spirit reflected in the affirmation of the interplay of the concepts of the inner light, service, pacifism, and mission. Raised in South China, Maine, Jones received a prophecy as a child: "This child will one day bear the message of the Gospel to distant lands and peoples across the seas."[4] He eventually enrolled in Haverford College, where he studied religion, philosophy, and history. At thirty, Jones took on the joint tasks of editing the *Friends Review* and teaching philosophy and religion at Haverford College. Jones taught for forty years at Haverford, where he inspired scores of students and young adults, including theologian, pastor, and spiritual guide Howard Thurman. During

---

3. Rufus Jones, *Pathways to the Reality of God* (New York: Macmillan, 1931), 199.

4. Rufus Jones, *Finding the Trail of Life* (New York: Macmillan, 1926), 20.

his long tenure at Haverford, he joined head and hands, and intellect and mission, as founding member and leader for three decades of the American Friends Service Committee, whose vision was to respond to the earth's most vulnerable people in the spirit of respect, affirmation, and pacifism as well as to promote peace and justice in the affairs of persons and nations.

Prior to World War II, Jones traveled to Germany, where he met with high-ranking Gestapo officers to intercede on behalf of the Jewish people. In his personal and public life, Jones joined contemplation and activism as embodied in the interplay of heart, hands, and head. He believed that spirituality illuminated our daily relationships and political involvements. Scholarship—the head—enabled us to share insights that awakened the spirit to its deepest identity as a reflection of God. Heart joined us with the heartbeat of creation and the pain of those who suffer injustice and exclusion. Hands were made for loving service and welcoming the stranger. Jones's vision can be summarized in the following sentence: "I assume that the major business we are here for in this world is to be a rightly fashioned person as an organ of the divine purpose."[5]

The Illumined Life

When my grandchildren were small, I used to sing them a song about the fabled "Mr. Rabbit," popularized by folk singer Burl Ives:

> Mr. Rabbit, Mr. Rabbit
> Your coat is mighty gray
> Yes, bless God, it's made that way
> Every little soul must shine, shine
> Every little soul must shine, shine.

---

5. Rufus Jones, *The Luminous Trail* (New York: Macmillan, 1947), 13.

Rufus Jones would have concurred with this song's message. Every little soul shines. Deep down, God's light shines in and through everyone, regardless of their age, ethnicity, religion, intelligence, sex, or sexual identity. Accordingly, deep down, everyone is a mystic. There is a seed of God in every soul ready to burst forth with the right nurturing, intentionality, and environment. Despite the reality of sin, alienation, and violence, no one is ever separated from God:

> Something of God, something of that high spiritual nature—the World within the world we see—is formed within the structure of the human soul, so that it is never, even though "born and banished into mystery," beyond the hail of its true source and home, and never without the possibility of divine assistance and communion.[6]

We can never run away from God's Spirit, because divinity is our deepest reality. Our hearts are restless, not because God is something for which we must search on the outside but because God is our innermost reality and deepest desire, often hidden by our own busyness, emphasis on consumption, focus on external realities, and acquiescent society's misplaced values and prejudice. The Beyond is within and gives life and light to every soul. Yet, the inner light is a dynamic, lively reality that fulfills, rather than diminishes, the human adventure. This is true not only for us but for everyone we meet.

Discovering God's realm within pushes us forward toward new possibilities for our lives and the planet. The glory of God is a person fully alive, as Irenaeus proclaimed, and in our encounters with God, we are brought to fulfillment, and "we see at last what

---

6. Rufus Jones, *Religious Foundations* (New York: Macmillan, 1923), 3.

man was meant to be—as we usually have not done—the divine possibilities of the human nature we bear."[7]

The Unity of Spirituality and Activity

As God's children, we all belong to God's beloved community. We are joined in a fabric and interdependence in which sacred and secular, contemplation and action, and meditation and justice-seeking are one. The calling of the mystic is to seek God's realm "on earth as it is in heaven." Indeed, the material world as the incarnation of God's presence needs us for its healing and transformation. In describing Jones's vision of contemplative activism, Kerry Walters notes that:

> The end for which we are created—the end toward which the inner light continuously draws us—is self-aware membership in the Body of Christ and creative partnership in the Kingdom of Heaven, that beloved community in which God's cosmic plan reaches fruition.[8]

In his quest for holistic spirituality, Jones distinguishes two interdependent types of mysticism: "negation mysticism" and "affirmation mysticism." Like the apophatic way, negation mysticism goes beyond finitude and personality to the Infinite and Impersonal. No words can describe the divine, nor can the world we live in ever satisfy our spiritual desires. In contrast, affirmative mysticism, congruent with the *kataphatic* way, sees the ubiquitous experience of God as the inspiration to healing the world. As Jones asserts:

> More important than the vision is obedience to the vision. There are battles to fight and victories to be won.

---

7. Rufus Jones*: A Call to What Is Vital* (New York: Macmillan, 1948), 109–10.

8. Walters, *Rufus Jones*, 31.

God's kingdom is to be advanced. Error is to be attacked and truth is to be established. Those who would have a closer view of the divine must seek it in the life of love and sacrifice.[9]

Affirmative mystics find God's presence in finite everyday life. "Nothing now can be unimportant. There is more in the least event than the ordinary eye sees. Every situation may be turned into an occasion for winning a nearer view of God. . . . The slightest deed of pure love is a holy thing because God shines through it and is revealed by it."[10] The affirmative mystic loves the world and seeks to form the world in accordance with God's vision. Recognizing God in all creatures, the affirmative mystic seeks justice and equality for all persons and is committed to healing the planet. If there is something of God in every soul, then every soul must be treated as a reflection of God. We must pray and protest. Resist and love. We must challenge injustice but see the holiness in those who perpetuate injustice. This engaged spirituality drives us into the world as God's partners in healing the earth. Seeing God in all God's distressing disguises inspires us to protest unjust political policies regarding economics, immigration, refugees, and human rights while recognizing the divinity in those whose policies contribute to these evils.

To many people these days, the United States and other liberal democracies are going through a dark time, dominated by the values of self-interest, vindictiveness, exclusion, isolationism, nationalism, and materialism. While we must oppose policies that disregard the divinely based rights of marginalized groups, we must also pray for our leaders that they might gain spirits of humility, compassion, and justice. We must look for divinity disguised by political leaders' values and priorities and seek to lure

9. Rufus Jones, *Social Law in the Spiritual World* (Philadelphia: John C. Winston, 1904), 153.
10. Ibid.

divine wisdom from its hiding places through loving confrontation and challenge.

This vision of God's universal presence inspired Rufus Jones to guide the political and humanitarian activities of the American Friends Service Committee, fight for justice for all people, and seek to liberate Jewish people from Nazi Germany. The call of God's light is to claim our vocation of partnership in healing the good earth and all its peoples.

Reflection: Joining Head, Heart, and Hands

Rufus Jones advocated a worldly and affirmative mysticism, grounded in his recognition of God's presence in everyone. Mysticism is our birthright, and mystical experiences invite us to move from individualism to world loyalty in our quest to heal the world. Our recognition of something of God in each person inspires us to seek justice and peace in the social order.

The Quaker spirituality, embodied by Rufus Jones, begins in silence, listening for the still, small voice of God. Out of deep silence flows compassion and commitment to change the social order to support the spiritual growth of each person and justice in our national life. Rufus Jones's affirmative mysticism inspires us to:

1. *Cultivate silence, opening to "something of God" in yourself and those around you.*
2. *Commit yourself to spiritual decluttering, living more simply to enhance your awareness of God and promote the well-being of the planet.*
3. *Look for the light in every creature and commit yourself to encouraging others to experience their own inner light.*
4. *Let your life speak in acts of reconciliation and restoring, advocating for social policies that help others, especially the marginalized and vulnerable.*

Spiritual maturity leads to political involvement. The *beloved community* is a term that Josiah Royce and later Rufus Jones and Martin Luther King Jr. used to describe the world as God intends it. A follower of the way of Jesus, Jones affirmed Jesus's prayer that God's "will be done, your kingdom come, on earth as it is in heaven."

In the beloved community, we live by love. We not only listen to our lives; we let our lives speak, through acts of love. We also listen to the lives of those around us, not presuming to know God's calling in their lives but seeking to support their opening to God's vision for them through acts of compassion and justice. In a time of war, we can discover the wisdom of a bumper sticker I saw during the Vietnam War: "Arms are for hugging." We can make a commitment to bring beauty, justice, and healing to every situation and reach out in love to respond to anyone in pain. Like Albert Schweitzer, we can choose to recognize the solidarity of those who suffer and then ease the suffering of all creatures by doing ordinary things with great love.

Action

Affirming the beloved community may mean serving meals to the homeless, building houses for Habitat for Humanity, tutoring a child or youth, or contacting your political leaders to promote justice, peace, and earth care. Jones believed that supporting the beloved community involves the creation of a truly just and moral social order. It also involves direct one-to-one experiences of loving kindness directed to the most vulnerable persons in your community.

Prayer of Awareness and Transformation

Parent of all creation, your light shines in my life and all creation. Your love joins us in one diverse community. Thank

*you for the opportunity to be part of your beloved commu-
nity. Help me, one act at a time, to bring love, justice, and
beauty to our world. Let me work to liberate the oppressed,
free the captives, and speak for those who have no voice. In
Jesus's name. Amen.*

5

Mysticism on the World Stage: Dag Hammarskjöld

It has been said that power corrupts. It has also been noted that the compromises necessary in politics and diplomacy deaden our spiritual lives. Indeed, most North Americans believe that the term "honest politician" is an oxymoron. The danger of privilege, power, and wealth is that you can, as Jesus said, gain the whole world and lose your soul.

While far from perfect by his own admission and willing to engage in the scrum of power politics, Dag Hammarskjöld (1905–1961) was universally judged to be a person of honesty and integrity. What surprised his admirers was the depth of his spirituality, as revealed in his posthumously published journal, *Markings*. Described as his negotiations with God and himself, Hammarskjöld's writings are a testimony to the impact of a spiritual leader's commitments to embodying their faith in public service, in which political policies are often a matter of life and death. Hammarskjöld was a hidden mystic, whose mysticism implicitly guided the mission of the United Nations from 1953 to 1961.

Born to Swedish political nobility—his father ended his career as Sweden's prime minister—Hammarskjöld was destined, as were his brothers, to follow in his father's footsteps. An economist, national banker, and Swedish representative to the United Nations, Hammarskjöld was nevertheless a surprising choice to be secretary general. Strong in spirit, he was highly intellectual, with academic inclinations, and seldom prone to self-promotion. Yet, from the very beginning of his tenure, Hammarskjöld was guided by a vision: "ours is a work of reconciliation and creative construction."[1] That motto became the inspiration of Hammarskjöld's leadership of the United Nations. He committed his heart, soul, and life to planetary well-being and was willing to contend against superpowers to seek justice and well-being, especially for the planet's most vulnerable peoples. He brought the United Nations to the center of the world stage by his mediation of the Suez Canal conflict and his diplomatic endeavors in the recently liberated Congo. His death in a plane crash over the Congo, as he sought to reconcile warring factions, was thought by many to be the result of the machinations of greedy colonialists, intent on maintaining their economic control over the Congo. In the spirit of Jesus and the prophets, Hammarskjöld sought to liberate the oppressed from superpower and colonial intervention so that they might live out their destiny as God's beloved children. Thrown from the airplane, Hammarskjöld's briefcase revealed several pages of Martin Buber's classic spiritual text, *I and Thou*, which he was translating into Swedish. Hammarskjöld's library and journal reveal a devoted soul who sought to follow the way of Jesus, guided by the principle "not I, but God." His inner life was sustained amid the maelstrom of international diplomacy by the anonymous British spiritual text *The Cloud of Unknowing*, Thomas à Kempis's *Imitation of Christ*, the writings of Meister Eckhart, and the Bible. Amid the storm of conflicting political perspectives, the threat of violence, and the temptation to pursue self-interest rather than world loyalty, Hammarskjöld found inner peace and a moral compass from his commitment to personal spiritual practices and self-awareness. His Christian mysticism enabled him to sacrifice

---

1. Roger Lipsey, *Dag Hammarskjöld: A Life* (Ann Arbor: University of Michigan Press, 2015), 113.

self-interest and personal bias and to dream of God's realm emerging on earth as it is in heaven.

ANSWERING THE CALL

In contrast to the other mystics described in this text, Dag Hammarskjöld's primary calling was to the secular rather than the religious world. True to his personal motto, *Numen semper adest*—the divine is always present—Hammarskjöld recognized that God's presence and guidance were both universal and personal. In the spirit of the Reformation affirmation of the priesthood of all believers, Hammarskjöld knew that every vocation could be a pathway to glorifying God and serving humanity. On Whitsunday, or Pentecost, just a few months before his death, Hammarskjöld wrote:

> I don't know Who—or what—put the question. I don't know when it was put. I don't even remember answering. But at some moment I did answer *Yes* to Someone—or something—and from that hour I was certain that existence is meaningful and, that, therefore, my life, in self-surrender, had a goal. From that moment I have known what it means "not to look back" and "to take no thought for the morrow."[2]

Although Hammarskjöld's writings are far from systematic, he is inspired by the belief that God's gentle providence flows in and through all things, providing the guidance we need to find our life's vocation as well as the vocation of the present moment. As Hammarskjöld noted, "the more faithfully you listen to the voice within you, the better you will hear what is sounding outside."[3] The pathway involves discovering the wisdom of "not I, but God in me," which leads to our recognition that we are the vessel and

---

2. Dag Hammarskjöld, *Markings* (New York: Knopf, 1964), 169.
3. Ibid., 13.

that it is the One who thirsts for our faithfulness.[4] God calls us to the Way of Possibility. Providence guides our steps, even as we are responsible for our responsiveness and agency:

> It is not we who seek the Way, but the Way which seeks us. That is why you are faithful to it, even while you stand waiting, so long as you are *prepared,* and act the moment you are confronted by its demands.[5]

Every moment is a holy moment. Every encounter, a call and response, and yet certain moments are definitive. Grounded in our openness to divine providence, these moments call us to choose life, transcend self-interest, and sacrifice for the greater good of those around us and our planet's future.

Gratitude

One of my favorite hymns is "Now Thank We All Our God." Written during a time of plague in which the composer, Martin Rinkart, conducted as many as fifty funerals a day, including the funeral of his wife, the hymn proclaims the wondrous providence of God, present even in life's darkest days.

> Now thank we all our God,
> with heart and hands and voices,
> Who wondrous things has done,
> in Whom this world rejoices;
> Who from our mothers' arms
> has blessed us on our way
> With countless gifts of love,
> and still is ours today.

---

4. Ibid., 91.
5. Ibid., 120.

O may this bounteous God
  through all our life be near us,
With ever joyful hearts
  and blessed peace to cheer us;
And keep us in His grace,
  and guide us when perplexed;
And free us from all ills,
  in this world and the next.

God's providence moves gently and sometimes dramatically through every moment of life. While God does not cause painful events, still in all things, God works for good to bring healing and wholeness to our lives. The forces of nature and our own immune and neurological systems undergird everything we do apart from our conscious decision making. Whatever we accomplish emerges from the interplay of divine providence and the intricate interdependence of life, reflected in our families, friendships, political and economic systems, and apparently chance happenstances. While tragedy and injustice are real, even these cannot overcome the essential goodness of life, manifest in the fourteen-billion-year process of "creative evolution," described by one of Hammarskjöld's philosophical mentors, Henri Bergson.

Recognizing his own privilege and the providence of God, in 1953, the year he began his tenure as secretary general of the United Nations, Hammarskjöld proclaims, "For all that has been—thanks!"[6] Gratitude is a state of mind, grounded in the affirmation of God's goodness and our role in sharing in God's vision for planetary well-being. Gratitude is visionary. It emerges from the experience of gentle grace, creative wisdom, and bounteous abundance, which are at the heart of God's relationship with the world. In the spirit of another of his spiritual mentors, Meister Eckhart, who identified gratitude as the primordial expression

6. Ibid., 89.

of a prayerful life, Hammarskjöld experienced God's grace in the changing seasons, the natural beauty of his homeland, the love of friends and family, and the spinning planet we call home. The mystic feels the currents of God in all that is good. He or she trains his or her senses to the movements of providence and discovers that a life of gratitude, manifest in generosity and care, is the only appropriate response.

SAYING YES

Our awareness of divine providence in our lives demands a response. And so, Hammarskjöld proclaims, "For all that shall be—Yes!"[7] In giving thanks, we say yes to our lives in their entirety, recognizing that within the chaff, wheat is growing, and within the pain, there is hope for healing.

During prayer time in many African American churches, a version of the following prayer is often invoked, "I thank you, God, for waking me up this morning. You didn't have to, but you did." As I hear this prayer—and now pray it every morning—I see it as a profound affirmation of the possibilities that emerge with each new day. God's mercies are new every morning! Great is God's faithfulness, and the One who has brought us here to this day will bring us home to everlasting life. In the spirit of the African American prayer, I invoke a version of the psalmist's affirmation, "This is the day that God has made and I will rejoice and be glad in it!" (Ps 118:24). Saying yes to God's providential movements makes all the difference in the world. It empowers us to activism, not passivity, and to agency in transforming the world to reflect God's vision. This was truly Hammarskjöld's prayer.

Somewhere on the mystic's journey, he or she says yes to God and yes to life in all its complexity and ambiguity. In saying yes, we focus our energy on the Way that calls us forward. We marshal our resources to be in alignment with God's will, to be a vessel

---

7. Ibid.

of grace in a challenging world. As Hammarskjöld notes, "To say Yes to life is at one and the same time to say Yes to oneself. Yes— even to that element in one which is most unwilling to let itself be transformed from a temptation into a strength."[8] The mystic discovers and then affirms that God is present in the whole of our lives, body, mind, and spirit; action and contemplation; strength and weakness; integrity and sin; and that God uses the wreckage of our lives to create beauty and love. In that grateful yes to gentle and unceasing providence, we discover our lives as gifts of God and our commitments as responses to a love beyond belief. We don't need to know the theological formulas, we simply need to follow with our fragile yet powerful yes. In saying yes, we find our Way, and then on the Way discover that God's providence has called us each step of the Way.

OUTER ACTION, INNER STRENGTH

Hammarskjöld asserted that "the road to holiness necessarily passes through the world of action."[9] Holistic spirituality joins contemplation and action. Compassionate action over the long haul requires spiritual depth to nurture the virtues of patience, persistence, and self-transcendence. As the leader of the United Nations, Hammarskjöld learned that he must "push his awareness to the utmost limit without losing his inner quiet, he must be able to see with the eyes of others from within their personality without losing his own."[10] This is what one of my professors, Bernard Loomer, described as stature, or spiritual size, the ability to embrace contrasting positions and empathetically experience others' viewpoints while maintaining your inner integrity and ability to draw boundaries. Spiritual stature enables us to move from self-interest and self-centeredness to selflessness and

---

8. Ibid., 92.
9. Ibid., 122.
10. Lipsey, *Hammarskjöld: A Life*, 5.

self-transcendence. As pastor and administrator, I've sought to live by the quest for spiritual stature, grounded in the recognition that there may be more than one answer to important questions, that more than one solution is possible, and that others are as deeply committed and thoughtful about their positions as I am. This spiritual stature enabled Hammarskjöld to state boldly his own perspective while valuing the positions of other international actors. Although Hammarskjöld recognized that there is no neutral individual, a person of integrity can act in a neutral and respectful fashion to all parties involved in a dispute. This is ultimately a matter of mindfulness, or self-awareness:

> The international civil servant must keep himself under the strictest observation. He is not requested to be a neuter in the sense that he has to have no sympathies or antipathies . . . that he is to have no ideas or ideals that matter for him. However, he is requested to be fully aware of those human reactions and meticulously check himself so that they are not permitted to influence his actions.[11]

On the world stage, in local politics, or church leadership, a commitment to self-awareness, undergirded by spiritual practices, enables us to find a center in the cyclone and maintain our integrity when we are tempted to pursue self-interest or let our biases affect our decision making. Large-souled leaders see the big picture, understand the positions of detractors, and look beyond present gain to the well-being of the community for generations to come.

Reflection: Mysticism on the World Stage

The world of politics and diplomacy seems the last place you would expect to find a mystic. Politics is often about power and position. Most observers believe that politicians tend to focus on

---

11. Ibid., 506.

self-interest, ideology, and nationalism rather than world loyalty. Introspection and self-awareness appear to be debits rather than assets in the maelstrom of political life and foreign relationships. Bloviation, doubling down on dubious positions, painting other positions in their worst light, and dishonesty seem to be the order of the day in the political arena. Cultivating an inner life and seeing God's presence in a political adversary is often seen to be a handicap in the hardball, win-or-lose world of politics and diplomacy. Political strength in a divisive world is identified with dishonesty, polarization, and inflexibility, as well as an implicit dehumanization of our nation's opponents.

Dag Hammarskjöld was an unlikely politician as well as a mystic. He experienced holiness in those with whom he contended. Yet, he could be unyielding in his quest for justice. He was not afraid to challenge powerful nations—the Soviet Union, Great Britain, the United States, and France—in the quest for peace. Hammarskjöld's persistence and force of character reflected a deep inner life, which enabled him to experience holiness amid the maelstrom of power politics and diplomatic intrigue. Hammarskjöld's intention was to "preserve silence with—amid the noise. To remain open and quiet . . . no matter how many tramp across the parade ground under an arid sky."[12] We can follow Hammarskjöld's spiritual activism by embodying the following practices:

1. *Make time for regular periods of silence as you seek God's guidance for your personal life and role as a citizen.*
2. *Practice gratitude regularly, giving thanks for the many blessings you receive daily and commit yourself to sharing these blessings with others.*
3. *Consider the great yes that calls you forward. Cultivate an awareness of divine possibilities in every situation.*
4. *Regularly ask the question, "How can I serve?"*

---

12. Hammarskjöld, *Markings*, 83.

In his inaugural speech as secretary general of the United Nations, Dag Hammarskjöld asserted that "ours is a work of reconciliation and creative construction."[13] The quest for healing involves the interplay of service and sacrifice throughout our lives. Healing acts involve the constant question, "How can I serve?" in a way that honors the equality and agency of others, particularly those who have been marginalized, and then, in response, sacrificing our privilege for the well-being of others. Sacrifice is a gift and a blessing, not a requirement. Those experiencing poverty and oppression are compelled to sacrifice by those in power. In contrast, those experiencing the privileges of race, sex, economics, education, and health are invited to live sacrificially and mindfully in their personal and political lives, and yes, all of our lives are political insofar as we help shape our communities by voting and by communicating with our government officials.

Action

Hammarskjöld believed that commitment to acts of healing and reconciliation, as well as acts of creative transformation at the local and global levels, involves living and acting mindfully. For example, in the wake of the United States' walking away from the Paris Agreements on Climate Change in 2017, I chose to be more mindful of energy use, to live more simply, to drive less, and to become more involved in the ecological well-being of Cape Cod. I regularly contact my political representatives regarding issues of social welfare, health care, and environmental protection. In daily life, when I find myself becoming impatient at home or tempted to balk at a request from my wife, I pause and ask, "What is the healing response?" The planet is saved by the acts of political leaders and governments; it is also saved one moment at a time

---

13. Lipsey, *Dag Hammarskjöld: A Life*, 113.

through acts of loving care that turn the world toward life rather than death.

In your daily life, make a commitment to notice healing moments and then act out of compassion and reconciliation rather than self-interest. As a citizen, be aware of governmental choices that tip the balance toward life or death, especially for those who are the most vulnerable, and act accordingly through a letter, call, or comment at a public meeting.

Prayer of Awareness and Transformation

God of all peoples and cultures, I give thanks for life's giftedness. Let my gratitude lead to creativity and service to all creation. Let me see your face in every interaction. Let your Spirit flow through my spirit in acts of love and healing. Amen.

6

Prophetic Prayerfulness: Martin Luther King Jr.

One evening after a particularly stressful and conflict-ridden day, Martin Luther King Jr. retired for the night. On the verge of falling asleep, he received an angry phone call, threatening his life and the lives of his wife and children. Unable to sleep, King went downstairs to fix a pot of coffee. King describes an unexpected theophany, or encounter with God, during his spiritual crisis:

> I was ready to give up. I tried to think of a way to move out of the picture without appearing to be a coward. In this state of exhaustion, when my courage was almost gone, I determined to take my problem to God. My head in my hands, I bowed over the kitchen table and prayed aloud. . . . "I am here taking a stand for what I believe is right. But now I am afraid. The people are looking to me for leadership, and if I stand before them without strength or courage, they too will falter. I am at the end of my powers. I have nothing left. I've come to the point where I can't face it alone."[1]

---

1. Martin Luther King, Jr. *Testament of Hope: The Essential Writings and Speeches of Martin Luther King, Jr.*, ed. James M. Washington (New York: HarperSanFrancisco, 1986), 509.

As members of the twelve-step movement and persons in crisis often assert, when you hit rock bottom, you may discover that you are standing on solid rock! King experienced God's voice speaking directly to him, giving the peace that passes all understanding: "Stand up for righteousness, stand up for truth, God will be at your side forever."[2]

Following his experience of God's still small voice in the middle of his personal storm, King affirms, "the outer situation remained the same, but God had given me inner calm."[3] Three days later, King's home was bombed. But King remained rooted in God's faithfulness. His encounter with the divine in the midnight hour gave him strength and faith to face whatever storms would lie ahead, not only in the Montgomery bus boycott but over the next decade as King championed civil rights of African Americans and called America to seek justice and peace at home and abroad.

Activists can be mystics and mystics can be activists. In fact, activism is often grounded in experiencing the holiness of our fellow humans and the nonhuman world. Encountering God in the wee hours of the morning energized King in the same way the encounter with God energized Isaiah, Jeremiah, and Amos, all of whom experienced a deep connection with God that inspired them to speak truth to power and challenge injustice and idolatry. We all need a haven of rest, a still point in the storms of life. Yet, out of that still point, we can find the resources to be prayerful prophets, confronting racism, sexism, violence, and greed, while seeking reconciliation with those whose actions promote injustice and polarization. We may discover our calling is to proclaim God's vision of Shalom in our families, communities, and political involvements. The sighs too deep for words, echoing deep in our hearts, may inspire us to recognize the holiness hidden in

---

2. Ibid.
3. Ibid.

those persons whose actions we must denounce for the sake of God's realm of Shalom.

In many ways, Martin Luther King Jr. (1929–1968) was a child of destiny and privilege. His father, Martin Luther King Sr., "Daddy King," pastored Ebenezer Baptist Church, one of the great African American churches of Atlanta, Georgia. The son and grandson of preachers, King was groomed to be a preacher himself. For King, the church was his second home. He once confessed that "In the quiet recesses of my heart, I am fundamentally a Baptist preacher."[4] His path ahead would lead to Morehouse College, Crozer Seminary, and Boston University, where he received his PhD in theology. Yet, despite his status in the African American community, he experienced the same racism that his less fortunate brothers and sisters encountered daily. King recalls his father walking out of a shoe store, refusing to make a purchase, when he was told by a store employee to go to the black section of the store. King also remembers his father countering the racism of a local policeman who referred to him as "boy" when he pulled him over for a traffic violation. As a young parent, King felt the pain of telling his children that they could not go to the popular Atlanta amusement park "Funtown." No doubt, King shared some version of the "talk" with his own children that today's parents of African American and mixed-raced children still must give their sons to prevent them from being unjustly treated or even killed by police officers.

We have come a long way since the 1950s, but even the election of an African American president has not tamped out the fires of institutional as well as individual racism. The rise in white supremacist groups, racist comments from government officials, neglect of persons of color in Puerto Rico, traumatizing of children on

---

4. Richard Lischer, *The Preacher King: Martin Luther King, Jr. and the Word That Moved America* (New York: Oxford University Press, 1995), 3.

our nation's borderlands, defacing of synagogues with swastikas, and the reality of white privilege call forth the prophet in all of us. In prophetic moments, we dare to present an alternative reality to unjust cultural, institutional, and governmental structures. Racism has been normalized by the "birther movements" and the comments of national leaders. The mystic, who experiences divinity in all creation, must counter the diminishment of any of God's children.

After completing his PhD, King and his wife, Coretta Scott King, pondered their next personal and professional moves. Although King had the opportunity to teach at prestigious northern seminaries, he and his wife, Coretta, chose to return to the South to pastor Dexter Avenue Baptist Church in Montgomery, Alabama. Shortly afterward, the city was thrown into turmoil when Rosa Parks refused a bus driver's demand to go to the back of the bus. Rosa Parks's actions reflected the pain and frustration of a community that had sought to be good citizens, fought for America's freedom in World War II, and kept the economy and white households going, but was condemned to second-class, separate-but-equal and, in other words, inferior status by both social practice and law. It was in the quest for justice in the Montgomery bus boycott that King drew on his spiritual resources to lead the community in the practice of nonviolent resistance.

Nonviolent resistance to injustice is grounded in a commitment to prayerful recognition of the essential unity of humankind and the experience of God's image as the deepest reality for oppressed and oppressor alike. Indeed, one of King's interpreters, Lewis Baldwin, asserts that "Prayer was the secret weapon of the civil rights movement."[5]Although King reported few dramatic moments in

---

5. Louis V. Baldwin, *Never to Leave Us Alone: The Prayer Life of Martin Luther King, Jr.* (Minneapolis: Fortress Press, 2010), 85.

his spiritual journey, the faith of his family and church and his growing sense of divine call inspired the prophetic prayerfulness that guided the civil rights movement of the 1950s and 1960s. He lived out his unique style of historically grounded mysticism as he sought to follow God's way in the scrum of power politics and advocacy for the least of these. His prayer life awakened him to God's intimate care and faithfulness and enabled him to see the holiness hidden beneath the hatred of those who perpetuated injustice or provoked violence.

King's prophetic prayerfulness, like the spiritual countercultural message of the apostle Paul, led to threats on his life, physical attacks, and eventually martyrdom. Still, hatred could not defeat his prophetic dream of God's kingdom, nor could conflict silence his critique of economic injustice and the Vietnam War. King's most famous words spoke of God's dream for a truly United States of America, living out the founders' implausible vision of all persons created equal and endowed with unalienable rights to life, liberty, and the pursuit of happiness. In this dream of God's peace, King visualized a world in which "sons of former slaves and sons of former slave owners will be able sit down together at the table of brotherhood . . . [and] little black boys and black girls will be able to join hands with little white boys and white girls as sisters and brothers."[6]

With the apostle Paul, King knew that divine power is present in weakness and grace is sufficient in times of trial. He embodied the affirmation that nothing can separate us from God's love. Just a day before his death by assassination in Memphis, Tennessee, King described a lived faith in God's companionship in all the seasons of life: "I'm not fearing any man. Mine eyes have seen the glory of the coming of the Lord."[7]

----

6. King, *Testament of Hope*, 220.
7. Ibid., 286.

THE SPIRITUAL FOUNDATIONS
OF PROPHETIC PROTEST

Many people see mysticism and spirituality as other-worldly in nature. Persons who experience God's nearness become so "blissed out" that they turn away from the messiness of everyday life and political involvement. Yet, nothing could be further from the mystical spirit of the prophetic tradition and Jesus's ministry. Isaiah encounters the living God in the Temple. Overwhelmed by his unworthiness, Isaiah wants to hide from Divine Majesty. Yet, when Isaiah is confronted by the question, "Whom shall I send, and who will go for us?" he responds, "Here I am; send me!" (Isa 6:8; see Isa 6:1–8). Jeremiah protests his inadequacy and inexperience, and then hears God's affirmation and call to confront the nation's idolatry and injustice:

> Before I formed you in the womb I knew you,
>   and before you were born I consecrated you;
>   I appointed you a prophet to the nations. . . .
> Do not say, "I am only a boy";
>   for you shall go to all to whom I send you,
>   and you shall speak whatever I command you.
> Do not be afraid of them,
>   for I am with you to deliver you. (Jer 1:5, 6b–8)

Seven centuries later, inspired by his encounter with John the Baptist and his experience of God as he faced temptations in the wilderness, Jesus proclaims the words of Isaiah as his mission statement as God's beloved Son and Healer:

> The Spirit of the Lord is upon me,
>   because he has anointed me
>   to bring good news to the poor.

He has sent me to proclaim release to the captives
    and recovery of sight to the blind,
    to let the oppressed go free,
    to proclaim the year of the Lord's favor.
                         (Lk 4:18–19)

The message of the prophets is grounded in the concrete encounter with God in the complexities of history. Prophetic mysticism awakens us to both divine and human pathos, or suffering, to use the language of Jewish mystic Abraham Joshua Heschel, who described his marching with King: "I felt like my legs were praying." Empathy, not apathy, characterize the impact of the prophet's encounter with the Holy One. The prophet wants to create social structures that enable every child to fulfill her or his destiny as God's beloved child. Prophets like King challenge any institution that blocks the path to any person's or group's quest to experience their identity as created in God's image.

While King never claimed to be a mystic, he saw God's providence moving through his birth, spiritual home in the church, education, call to ministry, and political activism. He knew that sometimes providence was gentle and unobtrusive, and other times, dramatic and seismic in its transformational power. He saw his own journey as a gradual and providential opening to God's calling in his life.

King was a prophet whose faith sensitized him to both God and the world. His prophetic spirituality was characterized by an awareness of (1) divine providence moving in history; (2) the dignity of humankind, grounded in the affirmation of the image of God in all people; (3) the interdependence of life, the single fabric of destiny joining all people; and (4) the beloved community, the hoped-for destination of the human adventure.

According to his colleagues in the movement, King tuned in to the providential movements of God by regular days of retreat spent in hotel rooms, when he would withdraw from the day-today conflicts in the quest for justice to pour out his heart to God. These brief retreats created sacred space for reflection and enabled him to have a thriving spiritual life amid the struggle. In praying in silence, King found justice, direction, and peace—the inner resources to face external violence, controversy, and threat.[8]

Partners in Divine Providence

How we view the world shapes our attitudes toward social transformation. If we believe that everything, including the actions of political institutions, is preordained, then social transformation is both unnecessary and impossible. If we believe that our leaders are chosen specifically by God and brought to power to fulfill God's vision, protesting injustice challenges God's will. If, on the other hand, we believe that the future is open and ambiguous, joining both the wheat and tares, and that leaders emerge as much by chance and choice as providence and that we have a role in changing history, then social transformation is both possible and necessary for those who follow God's vision of Shalom.

Martin Luther King Jr. rooted himself in the prophetic tradition of Amos, Hosea, Micah, Isaiah, and Jesus. He believed that God is concerned with this life as much as the next, and that God is the ultimate source of social transformation. Following Unitarian pastor Theodore Parker, King believed that the moral arc of history bends toward justice. God is guiding us toward the promised land of freedom, and God's movements in history inspire us to be dreamers and to imagine alternatives to the current injustice we experience. To dream of God's Shalom is to align oneself with the goal of history. In fact, spirituality finds its fulfillment in imaging a different world than the one in which we are currently living. In the context of national chaos, grounded in his nation's history of idolatry and injustice, the prophet Isaiah dreams God's dream:

---

8. Baldwin, *Never to Leave Us Alone*, 78.

The wolf shall live with the lamb,
     the leopard shall lie down with the kid,
     the calf and the lion and the fatling together,
     and a little child shall lead them.
The cow and the bear shall graze,
     their young shall lie down together;
     and the lion shall eat straw like the ox.
The nursing child shall play over the hole of the asp,
     and the weaned child shall put its hand on the
          adder's den.
They will not hurt or destroy
     on all my holy mountain;
for the earth will be full of the knowledge of the LORD
     as the waters cover the sea. (Is 11:6–8)

Eight centuries later, Jesus quoted Isaiah's prophetic words as his mission statement to redeem humankind: to bring good news to the poor, to proclaim release to the captive and recovery of sight to the blind, to let the oppressed go free, and to proclaim the year of the Lord's favor (Luke 4:18–19). The Jubilee year envisaged by Isaiah and announced by Jesus is still on the horizon and yet to be realized. God's dream of Shalom judges every political, religious, and institutional structure. The task of the prophet is to pay attention to the signs of God's Shalom, growing like the mustard seed in our midst, and to cultivate its growth by imaging and working toward God's new creation. Following another African American mystic, Howard Thurman, who spoke of hope as the "growing edge" in times of crisis and hopelessness, King asserted that even on the darkest night, we can see the glory of God on the horizon. Faith in God's emerging light enabled King and his companions to be faithful in challenging the darkness of institutional racism.

In their encounters with God, whether in the Jerusalem Temple, Birmingham jail, or a kitchen at midnight, prophets glimpse a reality that only the faithful can see. God will make a way when there is no way. God's truth will prevail. God's love is greater than fear and hate. God is moving, often anonymously and barely noticed, through the historical process to bring forth justice and peace. God challenges every political system and every political leader, even those we support, to seek justice beyond pragmatism and peace beyond divisiveness. Without a vision of possibilities on the horizon, the people lose their spiritual and moral compass and sense of hope. As King was to assert, "I believe that there is a personal power in this universe that works to bring the disconnected assets of reality into a harmonious whole."[9] With a prophetic vision, we can patiently wait for history's fulfillment and mount up with wings like eagles', run and not be weary, and walk and not be faint (Isa 40:31).

GOD'S IMAGE IN EVERYONE

At the foundation of King's theology of nonviolent social transformation is the belief that humankind's deepest reality and common bond is the presence of the image of God in each person, oppressed and oppressor alike. According to King, "There must be a recognition of the sacredness of human personality. Every human being has etched in his personality the indelible stamp of the Creator."[10]

Another activist mystic, Albert Schweitzer, saw the image of God in humankind—and for Schweitzer, shadows of this image are found in the nonhuman world—as the source of our reverence for life in all its wondrous diversity. This reverence transcends race, ethnicity, gender, nationality, age, politics, and ability. As the reluctant Old Testament prophet Jonah discovered, God is present in the diabolical and oppressive Nineveh as

---

9. Ibid., 91.
10. King, *Testament of Hope*, 118–19.

well as in his beloved Jerusalem. God wants to save foe as well as friend. God is present in white-robed Ku Klux Klansmen and in white-robed Sunday School children singing in the choir. God is present in those whose politics we support and those who seek to tear down the structures of justice we seek to protect. The vision of the *imago dei*, the image of God, enabled King, in the spirit of Jesus's challenge, to love his enemies and pray for those who put him in jail.

Reverence for life is at the heart of nonviolent social transformation, whose process involves the principles of (1) nonviolent civil disobedience; (2) seeking community with opponents, rather than humiliating or demeaning them; (3) opposing the forces of systemic evil, rather than individual persons, for whom we seek wholeness despite their attachment to structures of evil; and (4) cultivating spiritual maturity, a nonviolent spirit, motivated by agape, or sacrificial unitive love.

Our task is to awaken the divine in those with whom we contend by the rightness of our cause and by revealing to them our common humanity, and the reality that their spiritual well-being depends on the liberation of those whom they have oppressed. This vision of God's image in humankind inspires us to see God's image in ourselves as well as those whose politics and ethics we challenge. The oppressed no longer live by the negative judgments oppressors have of them as they proclaim, "I am somebody! I am God's child! I deserve justice and equality!"

THE FABRIC OF RELATEDNESS

During the quest for liberation in South Africa, native Africans were inspired by the message of *ubuntu*, the belief that we are all connected and create one another's experiences and destinies through our positive or negative interactions. In his quest for justice in North America, King championed this same vision of interdependence. We are not isolated atoms or rugged individualists. We are connected, even when we try to isolate ourselves from persons we deem inferior. God's presence in history and in the human spirit is the foundation of creative and liberating interdependence. When persons turn away from God, the inexorable impact of interdependence can also be the source of suffering and injustice. As King asserts, "We have made the world a neighborhood, and yet we have not had the ethical commitment to make it a brotherhood."[11] Still, beneath our false isolation, we are all joined as one humanity and one planet. As King was to affirm,

> All life is interrelated. We are caught in an inescapable network of mutuality, tied into a single garment of destiny. Whatever affects one directly, affects all indirectly. We are made to live together because of the interrelated structure of reality.[12]

No nation, no community, no species, no race, no individual can go it alone. We need one another to flourish as nations and persons: "For some strange reason I cannot be what I ought to be until you are what you ought to be. And you can never be what you ought to be until I am what I ought to be."[13] In an interdependent world, the most pitiable—and dangerous—person is the extreme individualist who goes her or his own way, assuming he or she can succeed without the support of others. "Me first" and "nation first" not only go against personal and national well-being; they go against the structure of God's world, where individuality and community, solitude and relationship, cannot be separated. From this perspective, the inner and outer are joined in the mystic's experience. In entering the depths of my own personal center, I discover my connection with all reality. I experience deep

---

11. Martin Luther King Jr., *A Knock at Midnight*, ed. Clayborne Carson and Peter Holloran (New York: Warner Books, 1978), 201.

12. King, *Testament of Hope*, 254.

13. King, *A Knock at Midnight*, 208.

empathy, which allows me to embrace the pain and joy of others and see their well-being as central to my own fulfillment.

The Beloved Community

In 1 Corinthians 12, the apostle Paul describes Christian community as a sacred place that requires everyone's gifts to be healthy and strong. In the body of Christ, our joys and sorrows are one. When one succeeds all succeed; when one is in pain, the whole community is in pain. Injustice to one group threatens, whether in the body of Christ or the body politic, the well-being of the community and the nation. The goal of our quest for beloved community, even when it involves protest, boycott, and political action, is reconciliation between oppressor and oppressed despite contrast and diversity.

In the beloved community, God's dream of Shalom comes to pass and the alienated are reconciled. This comes through the interplay of nonviolent, creative challenge, peacemaking, redemptive suffering, and the discovering that we are all God's beloved and all connected by God's gentle and providential web of life. Then we can all join hands and sing the words of the African American spiritual, despite our diversity of faith, ethnicity, politics, and religion, "Free at last, free at last; thank God almighty, we are free at last!"[14]

Reflection: Prophetic Prayerfulness

The spirituality of Martin Luther King Jr. is grounded in the affirmation that all persons are created in God's image. The true light shines in each person, even our enemies, and that challenge and conflict need not lead to hatred and violence. We are God's beloved children, sharing a common origin and destiny, grounded

---

14. King, *Testament of Hope*, 220.

in God's graceful and challenging world of relationships and the providence of God moving in all things, inspiring us to align ourselves with the moral arc of history. Let us live King's dream in our daily lives in practicing:

1. *Seeing ourselves as joined with everyone we meet.*
2. *Prayerfully paying attention to our attitudes related to race and our experiences of privilege, asking God to unite our spirits with everyone we meet.*
3. *Looking for divine revelations and opportunities for providential action as we view the news.*
4. *Prayerfully visualizing alternatives to the injustices in our community, opening to ways we can respond to injustice.*

Mindfulness is at the heart of the spiritual adventure. Seminary professor and civil rights activist Vincent Harding asserts that King challenges us to "pay attention."[15] Prayerful attentiveness awakens us to realities we often overlook, given our life experiences, education, economics, and social location. God hears the cries of the poor, but do we hear them? (Ps 69:33). God experiences the pain of the dispossessed, marginalized, and forgotten, but do we experience their pain? Do we know or care about injustice in our community? The prophet Amos warns that those who fail to empathize with the poor will eventually experience a famine of hearing God's voice (Amos 8:11).

Action

Given God's care for the poor and vulnerable, keep your eyes open as you drive in your community, walk in urban areas, or listen to the news. What do you notice in terms of attitudes toward the

---

15. Vincent Harding, *Martin Luther King: The Inconvenient Hero* (Maryknoll, NY: Orbis Books, 1996, 2008), 9.

poor, immigrants, and persons of color? How do you respond to people who differ from you? How will you respond to diversity in your community?

Recognizing the unconscious racism and white privilege that often shapes our response to "others," prayerfully pay attention to your responses to persons of color, persons receiving government assistance, refugees, and immigrants. What do you notice? Are your responses congruent with God's vision of Shalom? Do your behaviors promote God's beloved community? Ask God to give you awareness and insight with regard to your sins of omission.

Biblical scholar Walter Brueggemann described the prophetic imagination as the visualization of an alternative reality to the injustices perpetrated daily by those in power. Without the ability to imagine, to have a vision of the far horizon, we are doomed to perpetuating injustice, violence, inequality, and racism in our communities and nations. We must imagine a world of partnership and healing, and then let our dreams take shape in everyday life.

Remembering the counsel of Thérèse of Lisieux and Mother Teresa to do ordinary things in loving ways, in what ways can we imagine healing in the communities to which we belong? What alternatives to the current life-denying policies and practices of political and business leaders can we imagine, and how can we go about achieving these in everyday life and in governmental policies? Ask for God's guidance as you seek to bring healing to your congregation, community, and relationships.

Prayer of Awareness and Transformation

Create in me, O God, a new heart. Deliver me from conscious or unconscious racism, sexism, or privilege that I might walk hand-in-hand with all my brothers and sisters. Let me claim my citizenship in your beloved community. In Christ's name. Amen.

7

Radical Spirituality: Abraham Joshua Heschel

Abraham Joshua Heschel (1907–1972) has been described as a spiritual radical and the description is appropriate. In the common usage, "radical" means someone who advocates fundamental political changes and whose revolutionary views would turn the social order upside down. In this respect, Abraham Heschel was a radical. He saw the social order as broken and in need of transformation in terms of God's vision of Shalom. Heschel was once asked why he was demonstrating against the war in Vietnam. He replied, "I am here because I cannot pray." When his inquisitor asked, "What do you mean, you can't pray so you come to a demonstration against the war?" Heschel replied, "Whenever I open the prayerbook, I see images of children burning from napalm."[1] Heschel was driven by the prophetic vision of an alternative reality to the world's injustice and war, in which justice rolled down like waters and righteousness like an ever-flowing stream (Amos 5:24).

The word "radical" also means getting back to the fundamentals, the essence of life itself. For Heschel, the spiritual radical, this meant awakening to the living God who is constantly pursuing us and posing the question, "What will we do with our lives?" God, Heschel believed, is profoundly historical. God is concerned with the details of our lives and the social order. In the spirit of

---

1. Susannah Heschel, ed., *Abraham Joshua Heschel: Essential Writings* (Maryknoll, NY: Orbis Books, 2011), 17.

the prophets, God cares about health-care reform, immigration and refugee assistance, the growing gap between rich and poor, the quality of education, and life in the inner city. God rejoices in our celebrations and grieves with our losses. Accordingly, spiritual experiences plunge us into the maelstrom and messiness of politics, economics, and foreign policy. Mysticism, our quest to experience the living God, is embodied in political action and justice seeking. As noted in the previous chapter, Heschel described his experience marching with Martin Luther King in Selma, Alabama, with the words, "I felt like my legs were praying."

Born in 1907 into a line of Hasidic rebbes (rabbis), Heschel was part of the spiritual elite of his religious tradition. His father was the well-respected rebbe of Warsaw, Poland, and he instructed Heschel in the Hasidic tradition from childhood. When his father died, Heschel's family was plunged into poverty. Yet, this young child, then only nine years of age, continued to study Hasidic wisdom and became a brilliant scholar, whose interests as a young man ranged far beyond the religion of his youth to embrace scripture, theology, literature, and the social sciences. With the rise of Hitler, Heschel fled to the United States, where he spent the rest of his life as a professor, writer, and social activist. The flames of the Holocaust consumed his family, including his mother and three sisters.

Profoundly committed to the prophetic tradition, Heschel joined spiritual experience with political involvement in the United States, first as an advocate of the civil rights movement and then in opposition to the Vietnam War. Though he spent over thirty years in the classroom as a professor at Hebrew Union College in Cincinnati, Ohio, and Jewish Theological Seminary (1946–1972) in Manhattan, he joined head, heart, hands, and feet in the integration of mysticism, ethics, and protests against injustice. Heschel's social activism was grounded in the faith of the prophets, whose integration of faith and social justice was inspired by their experience of the divine pathos, God's suffering with the world. Heschel realized that God's vision of Shalom required our commitment. We are God's companions in bringing justice to the world. Moreover, in the spirit of Jewish mysticism, God needs us to be God's partners in mending the world.

Heschel saw religious experience as dipolar in nature. On the one hand, he was inspired by the delight, awe, wonder, and world affirmation of the Baal Shem Tov, "the Master of the Good Name," considered the founder of the Hasidic tradition. On the other hand, his spirituality was also shaped by the philosophy of the Kotzker rebbe Menachem Mendel of Kotzk, a spiritual iconoclast who fiercely demanded that his followers be honest, committed, and faithful. Integrating the polarity of kataphatic joy and apophatic starkness, Heschel lived out a holistic balance of delight and awe, radical amazement, and prophetic challenge.

RADICAL AMAZEMENT

At the heart of Heschel's mystical vision is the experience of radical amazement. In describing his own spiritual journey, Heschel notes, "I did not ask for success, I asked for wonder. And you gave it to me."[2] Wonder is essential to both spirituality and theology: "Awe is a sense of transcendence, for the reverence everywhere to mystery beyond all things. It enables us to perceive in the world intimations of the divine."[3]

Wonder leads to the experience of radical amazement at God's world. Created in the image of God, each of us is amazing. Wonder leads to spirituality and ethics. As Heschel noted,

> Just to be is a blessing.
> Just to live is holy. . . .
> The moment is a marvel.[4]

---

2. Abraham Joshua Heschel, *I Asked for Wonder* (New York: Crossroad Publishing, 1983), vii.

3. Ibid., 3.

4. Edward Kaplan, *Spiritual Radical: Abraham Joshua Heschel* (New Haven: Yale University Press, 2007), 203.

The practice of prayer opens us to God's presence in the world. In the spirit of Hasidic wisdom, a rabbi asked, "Where is God?" To which he answered, "Wherever we let him in." The practice of prayer "takes us out of normal self-interest, and enables us to see the world in the mirror of the holy . . . we can behold a situation from the aspect of God."[5]

Experiences of radical amazement take us out of ourselves to greater concern for the world and its creator. In seeing things from a God's-eye view, we experience God's pain at the suffering and injustice of the world. "Wonder leads to piety, and piety to holy deeds."[6] The reality that enlivens and inspires us is not apathetic or distant; God is not a changeless being but passionate becoming, intimately involved in the affairs of humans and nations. When we ask for wonder, we commit ourselves to embodying our vocation as God's partners in healing the world.

THE PASSIONATE GOD

For Heschel, spirituality is inherently relational and passionate because God is relational and passionate. Prayer is our quest to experience God. But, prior to our quest for God, God is in search of us. Human life is constantly confronted by divine questions. Ethics and spirituality involve how we respond to the questions and possibilities that God places before us in every moment of our lives as individuals and citizens. Profoundly embedded in the world, and deeply touched by our joy and pain, God has "skin in the game." God has a passion for wholeness, for Shalom, for justice in our inner lives and outer behavior, in the lives of individuals and nations.

Mysticism hovers between the *apophatic* and *kataphatic*, the unknown God beyond human fathoming and the God who can be described in human imagery. Mystics also straddle the theo-

---

5. Ibid., 60.
6. Heschel, *I Asked for Wonder*, xii.

logical fence between God as unchanging being, the unmoved mover, and God as dynamic becoming, the most moved mover. Some resolve this by distinguishing between the dazzling darkness of pure being, the Godhead, and the penetrating light of incarnation, God. Typically, these mystics privilege the unchanging over that which changes.

Throughout the ages, beginning with Plato, philosophers and theologians have noted that our images of God shape our spiritual focus. Many who conceive of God as pure, unchanging being see the mystical path, as did Plotinus, as a journey from the alone to the Alone. From this perspective, mysticism draws us away from helter-skelter of politics, economics, and domestic life to the stillness of monasticism. Others see God as the most moved mover. Fidelity to God involves immersing ourselves in the world of change and politics. While attending to the unchanging is an aspect of the spiritual journey, the role of the eternal is to give us a broad perspective and moral compass for our spiritual involvement. Wonder and piety, as Heschel notes, are completed in good works, performed in the uncertain and constantly shifting currents of daily life.

The philosopher Alfred North Whitehead discerned that the twin poles of eternity and change require one another and can be found in the beloved hymn:

> Abide with me
> Fast falls the eventide.

Twenty-five hundred years prior to Whitehead and Heschel, the author of Lamentations 3:22–23 highlighted this same polarity of changelessness and change in the Holy One and in our spiritual journeys:

> The steadfast love of the LORD never ceases,
>   his mercies never come to an end;
> they are new every morning;
>   great is your faithfulness.

The hymn and scripture suggest that although God's love is eternal, God's presence is historical, contextual, and dynamic.

Heschel coined the term "divine pathos" to describe God's relationship to the world and the heart of prophetic spirituality. God is intimately involved in history. God's joy and sorrow emerge in relationship to human activities. God hears the cries of the poor and suffers along with the neglected and maligned. God feels the pain of homeless families, farmers whose farms have been foreclosed, and single parents who live from paycheck to paycheck. God experiences the death of dreams and hope among inner-city children and Appalachian teens. God is rocked by bombs in Syria and laments the plight of refugees who are refused entrance into the United States and children who are separated from their parents at our borders. God's anger is kindled against injustice, because our injustice diminishes the image of God in humanity and destroys God's creation. God challenges the apathy of the rich and reminds them that their failure to hear the cries of the poor will lead to a famine of hearing the word of God.

> The time is surely coming, says the Lord GOD,
> when I will send a famine on the land;
> not a famine of bread, or a thirst for water,
> but of hearing the words of the LORD.
> They shall wander from sea to sea,
> and from north to east;
> they shall run to and fro, seeking the word
>   of the LORD,
> but they shall not find it. (Amos 8:11–12)

When we are inattentive to God's vision of Shalom and purposely turn our backs on justice, we limit what God can do in the world. We exile God to the sidelines, marginalizing God's impact on our lives, when God desires to be on the frontlines, guiding us in the paths of justice and healing.

The divine pathos is God's radical empathy with the world. God is in all things, in terms of God's gentle—and sometimes challenging—providence, but all things are also present in God, shaping God's experience for good or for ill. God is alive and relational, involved and concerned about what happens here on earth, and seeking justice in the everyday details of economics and relationships. According to Heschel, God reveals Godself

> in a personal and intimate relationship with the world. He does not simply command and expect obedience; He is also affected by what happens in the world, and reacts accordingly. Events and human actions arouse in Him joy and sorrow, pleasure or wrath . . . the notion that God can be intimately affected, that he possesses not merely intelligence and will, but also pathos, basically defines the prophetic consciousness of God.[7]

With Mother Teresa, Heschel recognized that we can bring beauty or ugliness to God's experience. We can bring pain or joy, life or death as our contribution to God. God's question to Isaiah and to us is, "Whom shall I send?" The empathetic God needs us to heal the world. God is in search of humankind and seeks to awaken us to the vision of Shalom, "on earth as it is in heaven."

Prophetic Spirituality

While there are many models of mysticism and spirituality, Heschel's unique contribution is his focus on prophetic spirituality. The prophet is one who experiences her- or himself as being encountered by God and given insights into God's vision for history, and who is sensitive to injustice and pain caused by the decisions of the powerful. The living God feels the pain of the world,

---

7. Abraham Joshua Heschel, *The Prophets, Volume 2* (Peabody, MA: Hendrickson Publishers, 2014), 3–4.

and those who follow God are especially empathetic toward those who experience injustice, illness, discrimination, or neglect. The dynamic interdependence between God and the world and God's own empathy with the world's pain challenged Heschel to seek justice and beauty both in one-to-one relationships and in the political and economic structures that shape our lives. There is no ultimate distinction between spiritual and political, individual and communal, in prophetic faith. Encountering God is not an escape from the messiness of politics and economics but a challenge to heal institutions as well as persons. Accordingly, Heschel's spirituality compelled him to march in Selma and to oppose publicly the Vietnam War.

For Heschel, like Jesus and the prophets of Israel, spirituality is profoundly relational and historical. According to Heschel, prophecy is "an interpretation of a particular moment in history, a divine understanding of a human situation."[8] In the interplay of God's call and human response, the prophet experiences the world from God's perspective. The personal God is always calling to us, and when we turn to God's way, God's vision becomes the primary lens through which we experience the world. The prophet is both a messenger and a witness, and her or his witness is grounded in the experience of God's call to heal the earth and its peoples. Prophetic spirituality shares in God's sympathy and pathos. For the prophet, each moment is decisive because each moment touches the heart of God.

Political and economic structures are especially important to the prophets. A decision made in the White House can lead to the deaths of thousands of persons, accelerate global climate change, and push the planet closer to nuclear annihilation. It can also save millions of lives and ensure the survival of animal species.

While the call to become a prophet to one's nation is rare and

---

8. Abraham Joshua Heschel, *The Prophets* (New York: Harper & Row, 1962), xiii.

involves a unique blend of divine summons, inspiration, and human response, each person is touched by God's vision and thus has a prophetic responsibility. As an inscription on a bench at Kirkridge Retreat and Conference Center in Bangor, Pennsylvania, counsels, "Picket and pray." Spirituality opens us to the pain of the world. Jesus weeps over the death of his dear friend Lazarus. He also laments the foolishness and hard-heartedness of Jerusalem. Amos, Hosea, and Micah feel the pain of the forgotten and marginalized, the tears of homeless farmers and starving widows, and that pain leads to lament about the nation's future and protest at its complacency and injustice. Spiritual experiences deepen our faith and our sense of God's presence in our lives; they also open our hearts to the pain of the world and the disparity between God's visions and our nation's actions.

Celebrating the Sabbath

To sustain their commitment to social transformation, prophets must take time for rest. Heschel and Jesus both saw rest and contemplation at the heart of reality. Following God's way involves immersing ourselves in human need; it also involves time for quiet prayer, family life, and study. Sabbath is at the heart of reality. Sabbath reminds us that the universe is in God's hands and not our own. God needs us, but God's vision will go on without our say so and may even be enhanced by our spiritual practices and times of retreat. We can be confident that, despite our foolish ways, the sun will rise again tomorrow and our planet will continue its circuitous journey.

Heschel describes Judaism as a "religion of time aiming at the sanctification of time."[9] On the Sabbath, we become attuned to holiness in life's perpetual movements. We dedicate ourselves to letting go of control, so that we might learn to praise God and to listen

---

9. Abraham Joshua Heschel, *The Sabbath* (New York: Farrar, Straus and Giroux, 1988), 8.

to the deeper voice of God within us. The Sabbath is more than a holiday; it is a holy day, a day of grace that inspires us to personal and planetary transformation. In stillness, we hear God's voice. In play and relaxation, we experience the deeper identities of our children, spouses, partners, and friends. We return to the source from which energy and insight flow. A contemplative day, the Sabbath orients and reorients. It turns us from self-interest to God's vision, and it gives us direction for the next steps of our journey.

Reflection: Radical Spirituality

Abraham Joshua Heschel embodied a prophetic mysticism, grounded in his sense of God's ubiquitous presence in the affairs of humans and the nonhuman world. God is alive; God is concerned; and God challenges us to live up to God's image within ourselves. God feels the joy and pain of the earth and its creatures. In encountering God, we feel God's pain and joy and are inspired to be God's companions in *tikkun 'olam,* "mending the world." Our sense of God's presence is awakened by the following practices:

1. *Cultivating experiences of radical amazement through taking time to experience the wonder of human life and the nonhuman world.*
2. *Regularly setting aside times for Sabbath on a daily, weekly, monthly, and yearly basis.*
3. *Contemplatively listening to the news on television or the radio, experiencing the humanity of those described and asking for God's guidance in responding to the pain you see.*
4. *Prayerfully considering contacting your political representatives and being willing to "pray with your legs," protesting injustice and environmental destruction.*

Heschel asserts that the prophet's voice emerged from his or her experience of God's pathos, or empathy, with the world. The prophet experienced God's suffering at the pain of the world and was inspired to challenge unnecessary and unjust suffering whenever it occurred.

Heschel also believed that social activism emerges from our sense of wonder and affirmation of the divine image in ourselves and others. Wonder and piety lead to social involvement to heal the earth. Heschel asserted that God is constantly addressing us, questioning us about our values and lifestyle. God is constantly asking, "What are you doing here? What's going on? And, how will you respond to it?"

Action

In our profoundly interdependent world, none of us can claim to be an innocent bystander. While we may not see ourselves as social activists, we can embody prophetic spirituality by making our use of the news and social media sacramental in nature. Go beyond the headlines and polarization to explore the real issues at stake, asking for God's guidance in responding to the pain you see in the media, with kindness and social concern.

Prayer of Awareness and Transformation

Help me, O God, to see the pain of the world as your pain. Help me to see your presence in all who suffer, and help me respond gracefully. Let me be amazed by this glorious world and seek to follow God's way to heal the earth in all its tragic beauty. Amen.

8

It Will Be Solved in the Walking: *Peace Pilgrim*

When I served as Protestant university chaplain at Georgetown University, one of the Jesuits shared a secret that shaped his ministry. "I regularly prowl the halls of the Law Center, trusting that God will direct me to people who need my services and that God will guide them to be where I need to minister to them." I took his advice to heart. For over three decades, walking has been at the heart of my ministerial practice. In my nearly twenty-year ministry at Georgetown, I walked the length and breadth of the campus twice each day, encountering students and faculty synchronously along the way. During my tenure as an administrator and faculty member at Wesley and Lancaster seminaries, I wandered about the hallways and seminary grounds, providentially encountering colleagues and students on my prayerful perambulations. Now, as a pastor on Cape Cod, I regularly walk up Centerville's Main Street, beginning at the library next door to the church and then up the street, as part of my ministry to the community. I pray that God will guide my footsteps and that along the path I will encounter those with whom I need to pastor. Just recently, on a walk through the library and then to the local playground, I encountered a dozen fellow villagers and congregants with whom I had meaningful conversations. My planned five-minute stroll extended over an hour! When I returned to my study, I felt a sense of God's providence in these apparently chance encounters.

Augustine of Hippo is reputed to have counseled, "It will be solved in the walking." This was certainly the case with Mildred Lisette Norman, known for nearly thirty years simply as Peace Pilgrim, who crisscrossed the United States seven times for the sake of world peace. I first met her in the early 1970s when I was a college student at San Jose State University in California. I encountered her again in 1980, just a year before her death in a car accident, when I was serving as a pastoral intern at First Christian Church (Disciples of Christ) in Tucson, Arizona. She was a white-haired woman in her early seventies, clad simply in blue jeans, a work shirt, and an apron that proclaimed on the front, "Peace Pilgrim," and on the back, "Walking 25,000 Miles on Foot for Peace." She carried all her worldly possessions in the several pockets that had been sewn on her apron. Her message was simple: peace will happen, if we seek inner peace and behave peacefully in our personal and political lives. She knew the path to peace wasn't easy for individuals or nations, but she also believed that unless we begin to seek peace one person and one encounter at a time, our world will be condemned to war and violence. Though Peace Pilgrim has been dead nearly forty years, her message remains an image of hope in a world in which national leaders promote chaos, polarization, and threaten nuclear war through tweets and name calling.

Born in the first decade of the twentieth century, in Egg City, New Jersey, Mildred Lisette Norman grew up in a typical middle-class American family. Intelligent and ambitious, she became a trusted administrator in a New York corporation. She had money, good clothes, and was married, when she first began to hear God's voice whispering in her heart, suggesting that she change her life. A few years later, America was at war—a just and good war in the estimation of most Americans—as our nation sought to defeat Hitler, Mussolini, and Hirohito. Yet, Mildred felt uncertain about the rightness of violence on an international scale. She wondered why she couldn't be a "patriot," supporting the war effort like her peers. Her spiritual and relational turning point came when she opposed her husband's joining the military. Both were adamant about their positions—pacifism, on one side, and military service, on the other—and this chasm led to a parting of ways. Though she was successful in business, Mildred realized that success and money don't ensure meaning and happiness. In response to her quest for meaning, she began to divest herself of her possessions and secured a modest position that allowed her to volunteer for the Fellowship of Reconciliation and the Friends Service Committee. This several-year quest culminated in her walking the two thousand miles of the Appalachian Trail, the first woman ever to achieve this feat. During this sojourn, she constantly prayed for divine guidance and that God would use her to serve humankind. In the course of walking the Appalachian Trail, she had a mystical experience in which she saw herself walking, clothed in a simple tunic, over hill and dale on America's highways and byways.

> I saw a map of the United States with the large cities marked—and it was as though someone had taken a colored crayon and marked a zigzag line across, coast to coast and border to border from Los Angeles to New York City. I knew what I was to do. And that was a vision of my first year's pilgrimage route in 1953![1]

She changed her name to Peace Pilgrim, sold her possessions, and acquired a simple tunic that read "Peace Pilgrim." She began her pilgrimage for peace at the Tournament of Roses Parade in Pasadena, California, on January 1, 1953, just five weeks after my birth in 1952, and walked every day for the next twenty-eight years, stopping only during the Christmas holidays to answer mail and respond to speaking requests. Her original goal was twenty-five thousand miles, initially to protest the Korean War and advo-

---

1. Peace Pilgrim, *Her Life and Work in Her Own Words* (Shelton, CT: Friends of Peace Pilgrim, 2003), 22.

cate for a Department of Peace, but eventually she quit counting
the miles, having well surpassed her initial goal. She carried no
money, refused contributions, often slept outdoors, and depended
on the grace of strangers for meals and lodging. Eventually she
traveled through all fifty states, having received plane tickets to
continue her perambulations in Alaska and Hawaii.

Peace Pilgrim experienced herself as constantly in God's presence. One night, as she slept on a bench in Grand Central Station,
she heard a voice addressed to her, "You are my beloved daughter
in whom I am well pleased." Upon awakening, she experienced
the world as a symphony of sound. As she walked, she felt like
she was walking on air. From that time on, the feeling of divine
purpose never left her.[2] Peace Pilgrim always felt herself connected
with her Divine Source that would never desert her but would
always be her protector. In the spirit of the classic Russian spiritual
text *The Way of a Pilgrim*, Peace Pilgrim experienced her life as a
ceaseless prayer, with God as her companion and inspiration each
step of the way.

God's Intimate Presence

The spiritual quest is grounded in a transformed vision of ourselves and the world. Two thousand years earlier, the apostle
Paul counseled, "Do not be conformed to this world, but be
transformed by the renewing of your minds, so that you may
discern what is the will of God—what is good and acceptable
and perfect" (Rom 12:2). For Peace Pilgrim, the world has too
often shaped our vision in ways that promote violence. Yet, to
this spiritual wanderer, violence only provokes more violence.
As I write these words, the planet is in peril. Not long ago, two
national leaders were calling each other names and comparing
the size of their nuclear arsenals like bullies on a playground.

---

2. Ibid., 41.

Playing with the lives of millions, national leaders caught up in a war of words threatened an arms race that could lead to a nuclear exchange that would kill millions and, quite possibly, lead to "nuclear winter." This is nothing new as nations privilege munitions over human rights and well-being. It is clear to those who seek God's peace that pompous speech and the ratcheting up of tensions are not the answer, nor can we secure peace by seeking first to objectify—that is, deny the full humanity of—those whom we consider enemies and, second, to threaten to destroy and then attack them. Despite the "common sense" and "realism" of the military-industrial complex and politicians who ask for increases in the military budget, while cutting taxes for the wealthy along with health care and services to children and the elderly, Peace Pilgrim and those who follow her believe that the only pathway to peace is recognizing the holiness of all creation and acting in accordance with that insight. According to Peace Pilgrim, "You are within God. God is within you."[3] Despite our blindness, we live in a divine environment and God is our deepest nature. We don't have to be afraid and fearfully scapegoat others, because we are always connected to the Divine Source.

Connected to the Source, to God, we are never alone. We have everything we need. We are protected and no longer need to project our fear on others or make war to feel safe. As Paul said in his Letter to the Romans, "For I am convinced that neither death, nor life, nor angels, nor rulers, nor things present, nor things to come, nor powers, nor height, nor depth, nor anything else in all creation, will be able to separate us from the love of God in Christ Jesus our Lord" (Rom 8:38–39).

Safe in our awareness of God's constant care in life and death, we feel confident to seek peace rather than war and love rather than fear. In that spirit, Peace Pilgrim walked the United States, trusting that God would protect her whether she spent time in a

---

3. Ibid., 2.

jail cell, slept on the side of a deserted road, or experienced the angry words of those who preferred the ways of war to God's peace.

God's Spark in Everyone

Peace Pilgrim once heard the voice of God whispering within her, saying "You are my beloved daughter."[4] She knew that God loved and constantly inspired her. She also knew that God loved all creation, and this shaped her every thought and action.

> I love everyone I meet. How could I fail to? Within everyone there is a spark of God. I am not concerned with racial or ethnic background or the color of one's skin; all people look to me like shining lights. I see in all creatures the reflection of God. . . . Every cell, every human being, is of equal importance and has work to do in this world.[5]

How can you keep from loving others if you know that God is in all things and all things are in God? God's spark is present in the leaders of North Korea and the United States of America. God is in the white supremacist and in those who affirm that Black Lives Matter. God is in the Christian fundamentalist determined to limit the rights of the LGBT community, and God is in the marchers at the Gay Rights Parade. We must confront evil, but also see the divine in those whom we challenge.

Pathways to Peace

Beating swords into plowshares and using atoms for peace is the result of spiritual discipline. It comes from a transformed vision that leads to transformed living and transformed political solutions. The pathway to peace is far from accidental but takes intense

---

4. Ibid., 41.
5. Ibid., 50.

and focused commitment. On the way, we discover practices of inner peace that can be catalysts for peace among the nations.

Peace Pilgrim begins her pathway to peace with the "four preparations." She believes that we must begin our journey by:

- *Having a right attitude toward life*—"facing the world squarely" and going beyond the superficial to the real.
- *Bringing our lives into harmony with the laws that govern the universe*—answering to the highest and best in ourselves.
- *Discovering and living in accord with our life patterns*—listening to God's guidance within and looking for God in all things.
- *Simplifying our lives*—finding a spiritual and material simplicity that brings harmony to our inner and outer lives.[6]

Next come the "four purifications":

- *Purification of the body*—eat simply, focusing on healthy foods whose production makes as little impact on the environment as possible.
- *Purification of thought*—positive and affirmative thinking, giving yourself healthy soul food rather than destructive, fast, and negative nourishment.
- *Purification of desire*—healing of desires to want what is truly good for you and others at the spiritual level.
- *Purification of motive*—self-awareness and mindfulness; purity of heart that leads to honest and loving behavior.[7]

Since peace of mind and action require letting go of what is superfluous and damaging, Peace Pilgrim counsels the "four relinquishments":

- *Relinquishment of self-will*—moving from the ego and its interests to awakening to divine guidance for the greatest good.

---

6. Ibid., 9–13.
7. Ibid., 13–18.

- *Relinquishment of the feeling of separateness*—seeing ourselves as part of a greater whole, God's presence, connected to all things.
- *Relinquishment of all attachments*—letting go of possessiveness of persons, possessions, power, and habits, and trusting God in every situation; this is the path to liberation.
- *Relinquishment of negative feelings*—letting go of worry, anxiety, fear, and placing your life fully in God's care.[8]

Similar to Jesus's Beatitudes and Buddha's Eightfold Path, these practices purify our hearts and minds, awaken us to our divine light and the divinity in all things, and harmonize our inner and outer lives to bring peace to the world. God will be found in the walking, making the world sacred one step at a time.

Reflection: Spiritual Pilgrimage

Peace Pilgrim touched the earth gently in her quest for peace. Although she was not a political activist in the traditional sense of the word, she believed that she could help bring peace on earth one prayerful step at a time. Connected to the Divine Source, wherever she walked, Peace Pilgrim was always home. We can be "home" too as we engage the following spiritual practices:

1. *Deepen your sense of inner peace through daily prayer and meditation.*
2. *Practice walking prayer, taking time to give thanks for the beauty around you and blessing those you meet. (If your physical condition precludes walking, practice this exercise by finding a beautiful spot in your line of vision and blessing every creature you notice.)*
3. *Thank God for the people you encounter throughout the day, looking for their deepest identity as God's beloved children.*
4. *Visualize world peace: see the earth and all its creatures as one living reality, permeated and joined by God's light.*

---

8. Ibid., 18–21.

Peace Pilgrim visualized a divine spark in everyone. She was thankful for every encounter and saw each encounter as a way of adding peace to the planet.

Seeing the holiness in others is an act of spiritual imagination. Accordingly, visualization was at the heart of Peace Pilgrim's spiritual practice. When someone was going through a difficult time, Peace Pilgrim reached out spiritually to contact their divine nature. As the divinity in her met the divinity in the other, distance no longer mattered as she bathed the subject of her prayers in God's light.

Action

In imaginative prayer, we are joined with all creation. In visualizing God's light surrounding and filling a person or situation, we prayerfully experience our unity with others and become agents of relational healing. Peace Pilgrim provides a structure by which you may choose to deepen your own sense of connection with the world and promote healing and wholeness for yourself and others.

> Visualize a golden light within you and spread it out. First to those about you—your circle of friends and relatives—and then gradually to the world. Keep on visualizing God's light surrounding the earth.
>
> And if you have a problem, take the matter in prayer and visualize it in God's hands. Then leave it, knowing that it is in the best possible hands, and turn your attention to other things.[9]

Such imaginative prayer opens our eyes to what truly is—the glory of God that fills us and all creation!

---

9. Ibid., 74.

Prayer of Awareness and Transformation

Let your light, O God, shine in me and through me. Let the divine spark in me kindle a fire in others and bring life and light to the world. In the name of the Light Bearer, Jesus Christ. Amen.

9

Contemplation and Compassion: Thomas Merton

In speaking of the mystic's adventure, in what is most likely an autobiographical comment, Thomas Merton asserts that the mystic "has advanced beyond all horizons. There are no directions in which he can travel. This is a country whose center is everywhere and whose circumference is nowhere. You do not find it by traveling but by standing still."[1] Thomas Merton (1915–1968), known as Brother Louis, surveyed the universe from the vantage point of a Trappist monastery in Gethsemani, Kentucky. For virtually all of the last twenty-six years of his life, Thomas Merton spent his days living monastically, far from the stormy currents of business, politics, and diplomacy. Yet, few contemporaries in the "outside world" had a keener sense of the struggles of persons and nations to find peace in a world of conflict. Merton's geographical world was small, but his spiritual world encompassed the whole earth and the depths of the human spirit.

In an interdependent universe, all life is connected. There are no isolated spheres. As Jonah discovered, there is no place to run away from God or one's true vocation. Moreover, if God is omnipresent, then every place can claim to be the center of the universe and a place of revelation. We can spiritually crisscross the universe

---

1. Thomas Merton, *New Seeds of Contemplation* (New York: New Directions, 1961), 81.

without leaving our hometown. Although Jesus never left Judea, he revealed God's wisdom and mediated God's path of salvation to all humankind. Centered in his native Athens, Socrates fathomed the depths of human life and glimpsed eternity. From the vantage point of the Trappist monastery at Gethsemani, Kentucky, Thomas Merton intuited God's presence in all creation and every human heart and challenged the leaders of nations to pursue justice and peace. Merton asserted that "our real journey in life is interior; it is a matter of growth, deepening, and of an ever greater surrender to the creative action of love and grace in our hearts."[2] Moreover, Merton believed that for those of us who enjoy traveling, "the geographical journey is the symbolic acting out of the interior journey."[3]

Today, we can see images from across the planet in real time. This morning, I witnessed the flood waters of a hurricane on the East Coast of the United States and the pain of those left homeless and seeking shelter. I viewed the struggles of refugees from Syria and listened to frightened undocumented workers fearing deportation. As I edit this document, my heart is broken by films of toddlers separated from their refugee parents at the US border. We are truly connected with one another, but our connection can lead to polarization, apathy, and violence, if we do not discover our inner spiritual connection with all creation through the interplay of grace and contemplation.

Born in 1915 in Prades, France, not far from the battlefields of the First World War, Thomas Merton was the eldest child of two artists, both of whom died young, leaving young Merton in the care of his godfather. As a child and teen, Merton and his younger brother lived in France, the United States, and England. His academic career at Cambridge was cut short by his raucous

---

2. Thomas Merton, *Asian Journals of Thomas Merton,* ed. Naomi Brown, Patrick Hart, and James Laughlin (New York: New Directions, 1973), 296.

3. Thomas Merton, *Mystics and Zen Masters* (New York: Farrar, Straus and Giroux, 1967), 92.

and irresponsible behavior. Exiled to the United States where he began studies at Columbia University, Merton found his way, first, as a Marxist and then as a journalist and English major. Raised in a nonreligious family, Merton was shocked when, in the course of reading a biography of the Jesuit priest-poet Gerard Manley Hopkins, he experienced a summons to join the Roman Catholic Church:

> All of a sudden, something began to stir within me, something began to push me, to prompt me. It was a movement that spoke like a voice. "What are you waiting for?" it said. "Why are you sitting here? Why do you still hesitate? You know what you ought to do? Why don't you do it?"[4]

Merton was received into the Roman Catholic Church shortly thereafter and began to feel a subtle but persistent inclination toward entering the priesthood. He continued his PhD studies with the hope of becoming a teaching priest with the Franciscan order. He considered the monastic life but found the prospect of becoming a monk far too rigorous and stark for his cosmopolitan spirit. When a friend asked him if he felt suited for the monastic life, Merton responded, "Oh, no! . . . Not a chance! That's not for me! I'd never be able to stand it. It would kill me in a week. I can't go along without meat. I need it for my health."[5] Yet, providence had other plans. Within a few years, he left his teaching post to pursue a new identity, that of a monk and later as a priest in the Abbey of Gethsemani. Despite the simple and disciplined life at the Trappist monastery at Gethsemani, Merton was encouraged to pursue his vocation as a poet and writer.

Merton's spiritual identity was shaped by the austere practices of the Trappist monks, more formally known as the Order of

---

4. Thomas Merton, *The Seven Storey Mountain* (New York: Harcourt Brace, 1976), 239.

5. Ibid., 293.

Cistercians of Strict Observance, a Roman Catholic order, following the Benedictine Rule and seeking union with God, through
Jesus Christ, in the solitude of religious community. A life devoted
to simplicity and isolation, joining prayer, work, and study, char-
acterizes the Trappist spirit.

Over the course of a literary career, encouraged by his superi-
ors, Merton was the author of over twenty books, including his
best-selling account of his journey from agnosticism to Roman
Catholicism and monastic life, *The Seven Storey Mountain*.
Grounded in his spiritual journey, Merton wrote poetry as well as
books on spiritual formation, politics and spirituality, and Asian
religious traditions. Though cloistered at Gethsemani, Merton
had a keen sense of world affairs. In the words of the title of one
of his books, Merton recognized that "no man is an island." He
was deeply touched by the reality of segregation and the complicity of Christians in both racism and the nuclear arms race. Keenly
aware of his solidarity with all creation, Merton preached a mysticism of compassion that compelled him to speak against war,
racism, and nuclear armaments. In the intricate fabric of relationships woven through all creation, our joys and sorrows are one.
True contemplation opens our hearts and breaks down the walls
of separation among persons and between humankind and the
nonhuman world. You cannot be a true contemplative without
love for your neighbor; and in our close-knit world of the internet,
cyberattacks, and nuclear threats, our neighbor is everyone!

In the final years of his life, Merton traveled to Asia, where
he met with Buddhist teachers and leaders, including the Dalai
Lama, who wrote about the encounter:

> More striking than his outward appearance, which was
> memorable in itself, was the inner life that he manifested.
> I could see that he was a truly humble and deeply spiri-
> tual man. This was the first time that I had been struck
> by such a feeling of spirituality in anyone who professed

Christianity. . . . It was Merton who first introduced me
to the real meaning of the word "Christian."[6]

In their conversations, Merton and the Dalai Lama spoke of
finding ways to deepen the spirituality of both Buddhism and
Christianity through sharing their unique wisdom with each
other. Just over a month later, in Bangkok, Thailand, Merton's life
was cut short when he was accidentally electrocuted while getting
out of a shower. Now, over fifty years later, Merton's global spirituality shapes seekers of all traditions as well as those who claim
no religious affiliation. Merton reminds us that Christ liberates
us from our false selves to embrace the wholeness of reality. In
silence, we experience the depths of God's realm within us, and
from that place of peace and healing, we can encounter our diverse
and endangered world with love.

The Universality of Revelation

According to Thomas Merton, God is alive and active in every
moment of our lives. Every moment witnesses to God's lively
and generous revelation to humankind. "God manifests Himself everywhere in everything—in people and in nature and in
events. . . . You cannot be without God."[7] In the spirit of Jesus's
parables of the mustard seed and the sower, Merton believes that
God is sowing seeds of spiritual transformation everywhere. "The
seeds that are planted in my liberty at every moment, by God's
will are the seeds of my own identity, my own reality, my own
happiness, my own sanctity."[8]

---

6. Tenzin Gyatso, the Fourteenth Dalai Lama of Tibet, *Freedom in
Exile: The Autobiography of the Dalai Lama* (New York: HarperCollins,
1990), 189.

7. Thomas Merton, "A Life Free from Care," *Cistercian Studies* 5,
no. 1 (1970).

8. Merton, *New Seeds of Contemplation*, 32.

God is constantly inspiring us. God's ubiquitous and lively revelation animates all creation. Contemplation is not so much the result of human effort, but our response to God's prior grace manifest in our unique, individual experience. Every person is touched by God. Despite God's apparent hiddenness, especially in those whose lives are dominated by self-interest and destructive behaviors, each life is holy and reveals God's vision for that person. We may turn away from God and lose our original unity with God and all creation, but God still seeks us. We know ourselves in knowing God, and experience divine intimacy in our own moments of self-discovery. Merton recognizes the priority of grace in the spiritual adventure. Our seeking God is really God's seeking us, sowing seeds of wholeness and meaning in our lives, helping us discover our own unique and personal callings. While God calls some to the priesthood and monastic life, these "religious" callings do not separate priests and monks from others. We are all responding to God's seeds, constantly planted in our lives, and each calling is part of God's plan to heal the world. God calls us to be activists, changing the world to reflect God's vision, whether we find ourselves in the monastery, classroom, or Congress.

> Our vocation is not simply to be, but to work together with God in the creation of our own life, our own identity, our own destiny . . . [to] actively participate in His creative freedom in our lives, and in the lives of others, by choosing the truth. To put it better, we are even called to share with God in creating the truth of our identity. . . . It demands close attention to reality at every moment, and great fidelity to God as he reveals Himself, obscurely in the mystery of each new situation.[9]

God meets us in contemplation and activity. In contemplative silence or action inspired by contemplation, we discern God's inti-

---

9. Ibid.

mate and guiding presence. We learn God's calling for us in our time and place, not just for our immediate circle of companions but for the whole earth.

THE SOLIDARITY OF LIFE

The universality of divine inspiration undergirds the spiritual unity of all life. We are connected. Deep as our contemplation may go, it is of little value unless it connects us with the messiness of everyday life. Deep within us, where we feel most solitary, we are joined with creation in all its interdependence. True contemplation opens our hearts to the pain of the world. Merton's own contemplative life led him to become a vocal advocate of civil rights and to challenge the nuclear arms race.

Merton felt the unity of life in a transformative way in a mystical experience on the streets of Louisville, Kentucky. On a rare outing from Gethsemani, at the corner of Fourth and Walnut, in the center of the shopping district,

> I was suddenly overwhelmed with the realization that I loved all those people, that they were mine and I was theirs, that we could not be alien to one another even though we were total strangers. It was like waking from a dream of separateness. . . . The whole illusion of separate holy existence is a dream.[10]

Merton realized that the most enlightened and most benighted persons were ultimately one. Monastic life does not separate us from the storm and stress of humankind. True spirituality connects because life is connected. There is no "other." In this moment of realization, Merton experienced great gratitude for the dynamic interconnectedness of human life. "Thank God, thank God that

---

10. Thomas Merton, *Conjectures of a Guilty Bystander* (New York: Doubleday, 1966), 156.

I *am* like other men, that I am only a man among others."[11] Merton rejoiced that he was part of the human family, the race in which God chose to incarnate Godself. There is no "other," for God meets us in every human face.

SOLIDARITY LEADS TO ACTIVISM AND PEACEMAKING

John Donne's phrase "no man is an island" rightly describes Merton's spiritually grounded activism and response to the diversity of world religions. Connected with one another at life's deepest levels, we are shaped by what happens across the globe, and what we do locally and as a nation shapes the lives of persons in Asia, Africa, Europe, the Southern Hemisphere, and North America. The fabric of relatedness, described by Martin Luther King and revealed in Merton's mystical vision on a Louisville street corner, demands that even when we are within the cloister walls of a monastery, on retreat, or retired from our professional lives we recognize our responsibility for the well-being of our planet and its peoples. Another of Merton's book titles, *Conjectures of a Guilty Bystander,* describes our profound relationship to the policies of our nation, whether in relationship to foreign policy and national defense or issues of justice and equality. What we eat and drink, our energy usage, and our buying habits shape the quality of others' lives.

In the context of the original unity of creation, isolated individualism is a heresy. The self-made person, whether individual or political leader, from this perspective, is the most dangerous and pitiful human being. Ruled by fear and self-interest, such a person views others only as threats and competitors. The incarnation reveals that "God is in *all men*. All men are to be seen and treated as Christ."[12] To do otherwise, Merton believed, was to deny "the most fundamental of revealed truths 'I was thirsty and you gave

---

11. Ibid., 157.

12. Thomas Merton, *The Collected Papers of Thomas Merton* (New York: New Directions, 1977), 380.

me not to drink. I was hungry and you gave me not to eat . . .' (Matthew 25:42)."

Contemplation, Merton believed, joins us with the least of these and compels us from our private meditations to join in solidarity with those who suffer and to combat the world-destroying threat of nuclear war. Now, more than ever, I believe, the prayers of contemplatives and mystics need to take shape in acts of kindness on an individual and political level. With the reality of global climate change, the growing economic gap between the wealthy and middle class and impoverished, the death of species, widespread famine, and refugees pouring across borders, a truly global mysticism that joins prayers with political involvement is a necessity if our planet is to be saved from destruction.

MANY FAITHS, MANY TRUTHS, ONE SPIRIT

A few years after Thomas Merton met with the Dalai Lama and Buddhist teacher Thich Nhat Hanh, I learned Transcendental Meditation in 1970 at an ashram a few blocks from the University of California in Berkeley. My journey as a Christian has been shaped by the insights of persons from other faiths—through Hindu Transcendental Meditation, Buddhist walking prayer, Taoist letting go into the flow of life, Native American "blessing way," New Age affirmations and visualization practices, pagan earth-affirmations, and Buddhist-Shinto–influenced reiki healing touch. Like Merton, my return to Christianity was shaped by my encounter with Hinduism. During his own time of searching, a Hindu monk, Bramachari, counseled young Thomas Merton to read St. Augustine and the Christian mystical tradition. Without our encounters with the wisdom of Asia, it is uncertain if the two of us would have become active Christians.

Merton's sense of the ubiquity of divine revelation inspired him in the final years of his life to turn toward Asia for spiritual wisdom. While he experienced the wholeness of Christian faith,

Merton recognized that persons of other faiths were also recipients of divine revelation and had much to teach Christians. Merton's death occurred in the context of a pilgrimage to meet Asian spiritual teachers. Merton sang alleluias with Buddhist spiritual guide Thich Nhat Hanh, and in an essay, "Thich Nhat Hanh Is My Brother," Merton asserted:

> We are both monks . . . we have lived the monastic life the same number of years. We are both poets, both existentialists. . . . It is vitally important that such bonds be admitted. They are bonds of a new solidarity and a new brotherhood that is beginning . . . on all five continents . . . and cuts across political, religious, and cultural lines.[13]

In our religiously pluralistic world, God's wisdom is revealed in all religious traditions. Accordingly, "it may be possible for someone to remain perfectly faithful to a Christian and monastic commitment and yet to learn in depth from, say, a Buddhist discipline and experience."[14] Today, we are called to be global Christians, looking for God's truth wherever it is found, even beyond the borders of Christianity.

Reflection: Contemplation and Compassion

Thomas Merton saw the dynamic interplay of contemplation and action as essential to spiritual growth. Without love, we cannot know God, for God is love. Our love for God inspires us to love our neighbors, not only those who are nearby but those whom we may never meet. Our love for our neighbor drives us to seek their well-being through personal generosity—acts of kindness and financial contributions—and through political involvement that

---

13. Cornelia and Irving Sussman, *Thomas Merton* (New York: Image Books, 1980), 151.
14. Ibid., 152.

supports our world's most vulnerable people and ensures just social structures that improve people's lives. Silence speaks volumes when it is incarnate in actions reaching out in love to the least of these. Accordingly let us consider the following spiritual practices:

1. *Cultivate silence, and join silence with your devotional reading, especially on busy days.*
2. *Immerse yourself in devotional books from a variety of spiritual traditions.*
3. *Affirm your unity with all humankind, looking beyond the differences of nation, ethnicity, sexuality, and politics.*
4. *Explore ways to seek peace, appropriate to your current political perspective. Allow God's grace to open you to new ways of peacemaking.*

Thomas Merton believed that God is present in every creature. Deep down, all humans experience divine wisdom. Our quest for peace inspires us to live our spiritual values in relationship to our neighbors near and far. Dutch-American clergyman and political activist A. J. Muste (1865–1967) once noted: "There is no way to peace. Peace is the way." Merton would concur with this statement. Merton called Christians to become peacemakers in their daily lives and political involvement. While we recognize the necessity for national defense and police departments to protect our nation and local communities, and while we recognize that spiritual seekers can have varied viewpoints on the role of force to secure social order, our goal should be peace in every interaction. In our fragile, intricately connected planet, the quest for personal and corporate peace is a necessity. Peace begins in our hearts and radiates to the larger community. Moreover, in an era in which political leaders threaten to destroy their enemies, spiritual seekers must put peace as a priority in political and international relations.

Action

Commit yourself to becoming a peacemaker, beginning with your personal relationships as you seek to bring love and peace to every encounter. Look for the holiness of every person with whom you interact. Look beyond any disagreements or sense of alienation with family members, co-workers, and fellow congregants. Recognizing the importance of peace seeking in international relations, look for peacemaking organizations that reflect your political viewpoint. Encourage your congressional representatives to seek peaceful solutions to conflicts at home and abroad.

Prayer of Awareness and Transformation

Holy God, you have promised, "Blessed are the peacemakers."
Help me see your world with the eyes of peace and help me
seek peace in every encounter. Deliver me from divisiveness
and polarization that I might be a force for peace and rec-
onciliation in every word and encounter. In Christ's name.
Amen.

10

Revolution of the Heart: Dorothy Day

In 2000, nearly twenty years after her death, the Roman Catholic Church recognized Dorothy Day as a candidate for sainthood. Some day in the future we may know her as "St. Dorothy." Despite her deep commitment to the spirituality of the Roman Catholic Church and exemplary acts of mercy, Day once asserted, "Don't call me a saint. I don't want to be dismissed that easily."[1] She recognized that saints could be categorized as ethereal and irrelevant to everyday people, so heavenly minded that they are no earthly good! Still, beneath her protest, Day believed that God called each person to greatness. "We are all called to be saints," Day affirmed; "we might as well get over our bourgeois fear of the name. We might also get used to recognizing the fact there is some of the saint in all of us. Inasmuch as we are growing, putting off the old man and putting on Christ, there is some of the saint, the holy, right here."[2]

Saintliness is not otherworldly but immersed in the hardscrabble world of social protest and care for the forgotten and vulnerable. In the wake of her death in 1980, one Roman Catholic

---

1. Dorothy Day, *Selected Writings,* ed. Robert Ellsberg (Maryknoll, NY: Orbis Books, 2017), xi.
2. Ibid.

historian described her as "the most significant, interesting, and influential person in the history of American Catholicism."[3]

Day would have noted that saints come in all shapes and sizes, some gentle and mild, others confrontational and challenging; some cloistered, others living in the center of the cyclone, navigating between contemplation and civil disobedience. Day fell into the latter category. Extroverted in spirit, she integrated her daily life with contemplative prayer, daily confession, morning Mass, and social protest. She even had an extensive FBI file, which included queries about the identities of St. Francis and St. Teresa of Avila. Her monasticism was lived out in the company of noisy, unkempt, and often unruly strangers, living beside her in Catholic Worker houses of hospitality and communal farms. Jailed many times for civil disobedience, she experienced God's presence in the belly of the beast as well as the quiet of the Mass. She discovered—like one of her spiritual inspirations, the Carmelite Brother Lawrence (1614–1691)—that while she protested amid the hubbub of the picket line God's voice resounded as clearly as in quiet moments of prayer and writing. She found Jesus more often in the poor than in the powerful and was devoted to the Roman Catholic Church despite her disappointment with the church's failure to side with the vulnerable and impoverished.

Dorothy Day was born into intellectual privilege in 1897. Her father was a journalist and one of the founders of the Hialeah racetrack in Florida. She enjoyed a middle-class childhood in San Francisco until the 1906 earthquake forced her family to move to Chicago, where initially they lived in a lower-class neighborhood, while her father was reviving his professional life. A reader and writer by inclination, Day set out to be a journalist and wrote prolifically throughout her life. Deeply empathetic, she identified herself with the struggles of industrial workers and the urban

---

3. Dorothy Day, *On Pilgrimage* (Grand Rapids, MI: William B. Eerdmans, 1999), 1.

poor. Like many socially sensitive persons of her time, she aligned herself with the idealistic visions of the Communist party and the international workers' movements. Her first journalistic position was as a writer for the *Call,* the socialist daily paper published in New York. Politically active, she was arrested for the first time during a protest for women's right to vote. In jail, Day discovered that it was one thing to have "theoretical knowledge of sweatshops and injustice and hunger, and it was another thing to experience it in one's own flesh."[4] Jailed for thirty days, Day's sense of privilege and separation from the least of these collapsed. Like the dispossessed and forgotten about whom she reported, Day felt the pain of meaninglessness and lost all feeling of her own unique identity. Identifying with her fellow inmates, Day experienced her common identity with those described as the nuisances and nobodies of the world. "I was that mother whose child had been raped and slain. I was the mother who had borne the monster who had done it. I was even that monster who had done it."[5] Everyone is both a saint and a sinner, and there are no innocent bystanders. We are complicit in the evils that we deplore; we are also called to be God's companions in healing the earth and its peoples.

Throughout her early twenties, Day enjoyed the company of artists, poets, and authors in the Greenwich Village scene. Though committed to socialist principles, Day often attended early Mass at St. Joseph's Church in Manhattan, many times after a night of drinking and conversation. In 1918, Day entered nursing school, fell in love with a fellow journalist, became pregnant and had an abortion to maintain the relationship, and then married a literary promoter and within months divorced him. In 1924 she published her first book, *The Eleventh Virgin,* and sold the movie rights for $2,500, enough money to purchase a seashore home on Staten

---

4. Dorothy Day, *The Long Loneliness* (New York: Harper & Brothers, 1952), 79.
5. Ibid., 78.

Island. A few years later, she fell in love again and became pregnant for a second time. Day notes, "I was happy but my very happiness made me know that there was a greater happiness to be attained from life than any I had ever known."[6] Still, Day often felt haunted and pursued by God, like the person described in Francis Thompson's poem the "Hound of Heaven." Religion for her was not the opiate of the masses, as Marx proclaimed, but the source of her joy and fulfillment. As she carried her only child, she found herself surprised at praying daily, even though she was unsure exactly to whom she was praying. With all her doubts about the otherworldly aspects of religion and the complicity of the church in thwarting social change, Day confesses, "I am praying because I am happy, not because I am unhappy. I did not turn to God in unhappiness, in grief, in despair—to get something from him."[7]

Although her common-law husband, Forster, an anarchist and atheist, disapproved of her turn toward spiritual matters, Day asserts, "I could not see that love between man and woman was incompatible with love of God. God is the Creator, and the very fact that we were begetting a child made me have a sense that we were made in the image and likeness of God, co-creators with him."[8] Though she had concerns that she was betraying the workers and poor of the world, with whom Christ spent his life, by aligning herself with the often politically conservative Roman Catholic Church, she became convinced that she needed to become a Catholic to deepen her spirituality and call the Roman Church to its true identity as a force for social transformation. Although she remained grateful for their relationship and the child they produced, Forster and Day split after she baptized her daughter, Tamar Teresa, and then was baptized herself. She was thankful

---

6. Ibid., 116.
7. Ibid., 132–33.
8. Ibid., 135.

for her youthful association with socialists, communists, and labor organizers, "who helped me find God in His poor, in His abandoned ones, as I had not found Him in Christian churches."[9]

From the time of her conversion until her death, Dorothy Day practiced a spirituality of compassion and justice. Regardless of the stance of institutional Christianity, she was committed to living out the spirit of the Sermon on the Mount—simplicity, poverty, hospitality, prayer, and pacifism. Following her baptism, she prayerfully sought direction as to how she might contribute to bringing divine compassion to personal and public life. During the Hunger March of 1931 in Washington, DC, Day retreated to the Shrine of the Immaculate Conception, where she prayed wholeheartedly that a way of service would be revealed to her. She wanted to "find something to do in the social order besides reporting conditions. I wanted to change them, not just report them."[10]

Day's prayers were answered with the arrival in 1932 of Peter Maurin, a French Roman Catholic social activist and spiritual guide. In many ways, Peter Maurin was Day's *anamcara*, a Celtic term describing a unique spiritual relationship in which another person mirrors the face of God for us and enables us to see ourselves as God sees us. As Day notes, "He sent Peter Maurin to give me the good intellectual food I needed to strengthen me to work for him."[11]

On May Day 1933, Maurin and Day published 2,500 copies of the first *Catholic Worker*, sold for a penny a copy. Quoting Maurin, Day affirmed that the goal of the paper was "to change the hearts and minds of men. . . . To give them vision—the vision

---

9. Ingrid O'Shea Merriman, *Searching for Christ: The Spirituality of Dorothy Day* (Notre Dame, IN: University of Notre Dame Press, 1994), 20.

10. Ibid., 23.

11. Dorothy Day, *Loaves and Fishes* (New York: Harper & Row, 1963), 13.

of a society where it is easier for men to be good."[12] For nearly two decades, they established houses of hospitality in urban and rural areas across the country where works of mercy were offered person to person, rather than in institutional ways. The Catholic Worker movement's goal was simple—to practice the traditional works of mercy, lived out by Jesus, the early church, and Christians throughout the ages: "to feed the hungry; to give drink to the thirsty; to clothe the naked; to harbor the harborless; to ransom the captive; to visit the sick; to bury the dead . . . to instruct the ignorant; to counsel the doubtful; to admonish sinners; to bear wrongs patiently; to forgive offenses willingly; to comfort the afflicted; to pray for the living and the dead."[13]

While Day and Maurin recognized the importance of institutional welfare programs, their mission was to see Christ in and receive Christ from direct encounters with persons experiencing homelessness, poverty, unemployment, and addiction. The poor needed more than a handout; they needed a hand and a heart. Throughout her life, Day sought to bring Christ to the poor by personal acts of kindness as well as through political involvement. She was active in the civil rights movement in the South and was arrested for the final time in demonstration on behalf of Cesar Chavez and the United Farm Workers in the mid-1970s. As Robert Coles notes, "wherever she was, she found time every day for prayer, for reading the Bible, attending Mass, taking Communion, and saying Confession."[14]

For nearly fifty years, Dorothy Day lived out God's compassion for the poor, grounded in her daily walk with Jesus. She never saw herself as other than those she served. Day believed that the movement must *be* poor to *serve* the poor. Trusting God completely

---

12. Day, *The Long Loneliness*, 181.

13. Ibid., 244.

14. Robert Coles, *Dorothy Day: A Radical Devotion* (Reading, MA: Addison-Wesley, 1987), 16.

for their deepest needs, Day and her companions saw themselves as living in the way of Jesus and receiving grace from those they served. She believed that "the greatest challenge of the day is: how to bring about a revolution of the heart, a revolution that has to start with each one of us? When we begin to take the lowest place, to wash the feet of others, to love our brothers with that burning love, that passion, which led to the Cross, then we can truly say, 'Now I have begun.'"[15] In her last years, sidelined by health issues and no longer able to run the *Catholic Worker* paper or travel, she confessed that "my job now is prayer."[16] In that short admission, Day models a spirituality for those who no longer can leave their homes to participate as agents of compassion and change. We can simply pray in our infirmity, touching God, feeling God's presence, and interceding on behalf of the world in all its tragic beauty. What would happen if millions of persons, confined to their homes, assisted living, or nursing-care facilities devoted an hour a day for prayer, such as the Jesus Prayer, "Lord have mercy upon me, a sinner," or visualized God's light permeating places of fear and pain? I believe that our world would be transformed and come nearer to embodying Jesus's prayer that God's realm come "on earth as it is in heaven."

RADICAL INCARNATION

Dorothy Day's spirituality was incarnational, relational, and vocational. Her spirituality inspired her to become a political radical. She sided with the poor and imagined a society in which wealth was distributed fairly. She took seriously the message of the Sermon on the Mount and the economics of the early church and believed Christian simplicity could be embodied in daily life. She chose voluntary poverty as a means of solidarity with the poor and

---

15. Day, *Loaves and Fishes,* 210.
16. Ellsberg, *Dorothy Day: Selected Writings,* xl.

to ensure the well-being of the most vulnerable members of society. While she was an orthodox Roman Catholic in many ways, participating in daily Mass, prayers, and confession, her orthodoxy was profoundly incarnational. The Eucharist, the body and blood of Jesus, as she understood it, binds God to earth and divinizes humankind. Her spirituality was grounded in a literal understanding of the words of Matthew 25:34–40:

> Then the king will say to those at his right hand, "Come, you that are blessed by my Father, inherit the kingdom prepared for you from the foundation of the world; for I was hungry and you gave me food, I was thirsty and you gave me something to drink, I was a stranger and you welcomed me, I was naked and you gave me clothing, I was sick and you took care of me, I was in prison and you visited me." Then the righteous will answer him, "Lord, when was it that we saw you hungry and gave you food, or thirsty and gave you something to drink? And when was it that we saw you a stranger and welcomed you, or naked and gave you clothing? And when was it that we saw you sick or in prison and visited you?" And the king will answer them, "Truly I tell you, just as you did it to one of the least of these who are members of my family, you did it to me."

Christ is in the "least of these." More than that, Day asserted that Christ *is* the least of these. According to Day, "The mystery of the poor is this: That they are Jesus, and that what you do for them, you do for Him."[17] The incarnation, as made flesh in the life of Jesus and the Eucharist, makes the whole world divine in nature. Incarnation reminds us to see everyone with the eyes of Christ and treat everyone as Christ embodied. In jail, Day discov-

---

17. Day, *On Pilgrimage*, 33.

ered that "Jesus is the fat lady. Jesus is this unfortunate girl, Jackie, who is making advances. Jesus is Baby Doll, her cellmate."[18]

Saintliness joins vision and action. The saints of the world—and remember that Dorothy Day called for common people to become saintly—experience God's presence in unlikely places and bring forth the holiness disguised by anger, poverty, addiction, and pain. While recognizing her own impatience and imperfection, Day sought to "talk to the men as though they were angels."[19] Deep spirituality lives with the creative tension of God's transcendence and immanence. The God of billions of galaxies is also our closest companion, addressing us by name and coming to us in refugee children, single parents on welfare, undocumented workers, and unemployed union members. Moments of transcendence remind us to be humble. Experiences of divine immanence inspire us to listen for God's voice in our hearts, our quests for justice, and the cries of the poor. Day avers, "On the one hand, He is closer than the air we breathe, and on the other, we are the grain of sand on the seashore, lost in the nothingness before the All-powerful."[20] Despite our apparent nothingness in the scheme of things, we are, as Psalm 8 proclaims, a little lower than the Divine and can do great things despite our meager resources.

Empathetic Relationality

Dorothy Day discovered the mystical body of Christ in Eucharistic participation in Christ's body and blood. She also experienced the interconnectedness of Christ's mystical body in human relationships. In the spirit of 1 Corinthians 12:26, she recognized that within Christ's body, "If one member suffers, all suffer together

---

18. Dorothy Day, "We Plead Guilty," *Commonweal* 67 (December 27, 1957): 330.

19. Dorothy Day, *House of Hospitality* (New York: Sheed & Ward, 1939).

20. Dorothy Day, *Therese* (Notre Dame, IN: Fides Publishers, 1960).

with it; if one member is honored, all rejoice together with it." In an interdependent world, the walls of separation between the rich and the poor, the privileged and the marginalized, and the citizen and the immigrant, are illusory. In the quest for a heart large enough to embrace the forgotten and vulnerable, Day experienced the deep empathy of Jesus, who wept at the death of Lazarus, grieved over the waywardness of Jerusalem, and chose the way of the cross, suffering on behalf of persons like ourselves, as the path of salvation for humankind. In the mystical body of Christ, there is no "other." Divine empathy reminded her that within God's earthly body, "I was no longer a young girl, part of a radical movement seeking justice for those oppressed; I was the oppressed. I was that drug addict, screaming and tossing in her cell, beating her head against the wall."[21]

Spiritual growth involves deepening our connections with others rather than retreating to solitude. Solitary moments of prayer and meditation drive us into the world, attentive to the pain of others as if it is our own pain and recognizing that God grieves with those who suffer. Relational empathy enlarges our hearts and inspires us to acts of mercy and justice seeking. Our sense of solidarity with the oppressed challenges us to respond to their pain, but also, as Day asserts, to prevent further pain and degradation by changing structures of injustice and inequality.

SAVED BY SMALL ACTIONS

Jewish mysticism asserts that when you save one soul, you save the world. This same spirit was at the heart of Dorothy Day's and Peter Maurin's vision of the Catholic Worker movement. While Day and Maurin publicly protested against social and political injustice, much of their daily work addressed the immediate needs of persons experiencing homelessness, poverty, and unemploy-

---

21. Day, *On Pilgrimage*, 5.

ment on a one-to-one interpersonal basis. Day believed that healing emerged out of loving relationships, in which the Christ in me
addressed the Christ in you. Following Russian philosopher and
novelist Fyodor Dostoevsky, Day believed that the world is saved
by beauty—the beauty of sunsets and children playing, the beauty
of loving relationships that bring out the divinity in ourselves and
others, the beauty of a smiling face on the bread line. In bringing
love to unloving situations, we bring beauty to what would otherwise be ugly, and bring joy to the lost and lonely.

Day's youthful commitment to union organizing and socialist
principles remained important to her all her life but was transformed into Christian principles of good and life-supporting work.
The Catholic Worker movement was inspired by the Benedictine
interplay of work and prayer. Good work is essential to human
flourishing. What we do shapes the world and it also shapes our
relationship with God and one another. Day would likely have
agreed with the Buddhist counsel of right livelihood in her affirmation of the spiritual necessity and ethical requirements of work.
Creative and socially beneficial work ennobles the worker, while
life-destroying work contracts our spirits. Good work enables us
to become co-creators, along with God, in bringing beauty to the
world.

Day believed that work was inherently moral. What we do,
how we do it, and the conditions in which we work reflect and
shape our spiritual lives. Work can deepen, or detract from, our
relationship with God and one another. In considering our work,
she wrote, "if these jobs do not contribute to the common good,
we pray God for the grace to give them up. Have they to do with
shelter, food, clothing? Have they to do with works of mercy?"[22]

Day recognized that simple actions done with love can change
the world. Good work, done for God's glory and the well-being
of others, participates in God's creativity, enlarges our spirits, and

---

22. Ibid., 248.

brings beauty to the world. Following Thérèse of Lisieux, Day affirmed that her vocation was to "increase the sum total of the love of God in the world by every minute act, every suffering, every movement of her body and soul, done for the love of God."[23]

Reflection: Heart-Filled Revolution

Dorothy Day challenged persons of privilege to see the world with the eyes of Christ and to discover Christ in the neglected and scorned. When we say that God is omnipresent, we assert that God is found in the least of these. When we proclaim the reality of God's grace, we commit ourselves to share grace with the marginalized. When we speak of God's omniscience, we affirm that God experiences our suffering and that our response to the least of these shapes God's own experience of the world and energizes us, in the words of Mother Teresa, to do something beautiful for God. In that spirit:

1. *Daily open to the holiness of every person, awakening to the needs of those around you, and quietly asking, "God, enlarge my soul so that I may serve."*
2. *Thank God for those unknown people, such as those who pick fruit and vegetables, clean your hotel room, and ensure your safety.*
3. *Daily contemplate the Psalms as part of your devotional life, beginning with Psalms 8, 22, 46, 98, 100, 139, 148.*
4. *Pray for our political leaders and the leaders of other nations, asking for God's wisdom to guide them.*

Dorothy Day immersed herself in the media of her time, both as a reader and a publisher. She recognized the power of media to shape our lives and political perspectives. For many of us, the daily news is often a source of anger and anxiety. Seeing the face of a

---

23. Day, *Selected Writings*, 274.

political leader we oppose can fill us with rage. Seeing the faces of the poor can fill us with despair. The problems are so large and our resources seem meager by comparison. Yet, our awareness of the pain of the world can inspire us to move from apathy to empathy when we open our hearts to God's compassionate companionship.

Action

As I've noted throughout this text, it is important to pray as you interact with the media, whether social, print, or televised. If you watch the news regularly, let what you see, read, or hear be a call to prayer. View a variety of news sources—especially those such as BBC, NPR, Radio Pacifica, and PBS—that turn our attention beyond North American issues. Let local news awaken you to the suffering present in your neighborhood, and let national and world news sensitize you to the pain of refugees, the faces of hunger and political oppression, and the victims of natural disasters. Pray for wisdom in responding to injustice, knowing that God has the whole world in God's hands. Pray for insight in confronting evil, knowing that your agency is essential for God's will to be done on earth as it is in heaven. Let your prayers take shape in acts of mercy and kindness locally and globally or personally and politically.

Prayer of Awareness and Transformation

Let my life be a prayer, O God. Let me listen to the cries of the poor and the despair of the homeless. Let me feel the fear of the refugee and the hopelessness of those whose cries have gone unheard. Expand my heart and love, and give me hands to help. In Jesus's name. Amen.

11

Conversion of the Heart: Óscar Romero

There are no norms for the mystical journey. Mystics come in all sizes, shapes, cultures, and personalities. Encountering the Holy does not lead to uniformity or homogeneity but to glorious diversity and individuality in which we become fully ourselves and fully alive in relationship with God and others. Nor are there norms for spiritual transformation. Conversion comes in as many forms as there are seekers. Sought or avoided, God may show up in a way that changes everything. Among the evangelicals, where I first experienced God as a living reality, a datable spiritual experience of "coming to Jesus" was considered necessary for spiritual maturity and, to some, salvation. Salvation, in their minds, involved eternal life in companionship with Jesus and our loved ones. At age nine, I came forward at a revival meeting, sponsored by our Baptist church, accepted Jesus as my personal savior, and was baptized the following Sunday. Little did I know the many twists and turns that would occur over nearly sixty years as I have sought to discern God's continuing call in my life. Like the vows a couple makes at a wedding ceremony, our conversion experiences are the beginning of a holy adventure and not a final resting place.

Other persons experience God gradually as divine providence unfolds gently yet persistently in their lives. In my own congregation on Cape Cod, we assume that the process of conversion begins at birth. Each infant is God's beloved child, and the baptism of infants is a sign of God's grace prior to any affirmation of faith. That childlike faith matures, often imperceptibly, over a lifetime. Salvation involves both heaven and earth, and both the ebb and flow of history and everlasting life.

I have come to believe that God works through both dramatic and subtle spiritual experiences. Although I accepted Jesus as savior as a child, I began a new path toward spiritual maturity in college when, after leaving the church for a few years, I learned Transcendental Meditation, a Hindu-based spiritual practice, and then, without any drama, returned to church the next week. God calls to us in a variety of ways, depending on our current personal and social context, and every deep spiritual experience is legitimate. The true light, as John's Gospel proclaims, enlightens all persons.

Still, there are times when God comes to us unexpectedly and forcefully, turning our world upside down and virtually compelling us to change course, claiming a new identity and vocation. On the road to Damascus, Saul of Tarsus experienced a blinding light and heard the voice of Christ, calling him to a new life and giving him a new vocation as an apostle of Jesus Christ. With this vocation as apostle to the whole earth came a new birth and new name, Paul. Blinded by God's light, Paul experienced a new vision of reality and embraced the Christ whose followers he had previously persecuted.

Nineteen hundred years later, Archbishop Óscar Romero (now Saint Óscar Romero), the moderate, introverted, apolitical leader of the El Salvadoran Roman Catholic Church, experienced a similar spiritual crisis in response to the assassination of his dear friend and fellow priest Rutilio Grande. As liberation theologian Jon Sobrino notes, Romero, who prior to that time opposed Grande's left-wing "politicization" of the church, experienced a profound conversion of heart and mind: "I think that, as Archbishop Romero stood gazing at the mortal remains of Rutilio Grande, the scales fell from his eyes. Rutilio had been right! The kind of pastoral activity, the kind of church, the kind of faith he had advocated had been the right kind after all."[1] Romero realized that it was not enough to feed the poor; to be faithful to the gospel, he must advocate for social justice and political change to ensure that the poor can produce their own food and determine their own economic destinies. Romero discovered that peace in the streets, grounded in enforced law and order, was insufficient to secure God's realm. Peace must be grounded in equality and justice that enables the poor to experience the dignity of self-determination, economic well-being, and personal dignity as God's beloved children. In that moment of transformation—and this moment might have been the culmination of God's quiet providence working in Romero's life over many years—the archbishop who had previously felt at home among the wealthy and powerful, thinking that encouraging their generosity toward the church and its missions was more important than changing the social order, experienced the wisdom of African American mystic and theologian Howard Thurman:

> To those who need profound succor and strength to enable them to live in the present with dignity and creativity, Christianity has often been sterile and of little avail. . . . Too often the price exacted by society for security and respectability is that the Christian movement in its formal expression must be on the side of the strong against the weak. This is a matter of tremendous significance, for it reveals to what extent a religion that was born

---

1. Jon Sobrino, *Archbishop Romero: Memories and Reflections* (Maryknoll, NY: Orbis Books, 2016), 8.

of a people acquainted with persecution and suffering has become the cornerstone of a civilization and of nations whose very position in modern life has been secured by the ruthless use of power applied to weak and defenseless peoples.[2]

Perhaps, at that moment, Romero experienced deep in his spirit the meaning of the apostle Paul's counsel, "Do not be conformed to this world, but be transformed by the renewing of your minds, so that you may discern what is the will of God—what is good and acceptable and perfect" (Rom 12:2). As the scales fell from his eyes, Romero may have realized that he needed to break free from his close ties with the wealthy and powerful to experience God's will for him as archbishop of the poor as well as the wealthy.

Óscar Romero (1917–1980) was an unlikely spiritual revolutionary. Although he was raised among the working class— his father was postmaster and telegraph operator in a rural El Salvadoran village—Romero, from the very beginning, understood religion in terms of personal piety and one-to-one relational generosity. Groomed to be a tradesman by his father, Romero spent his free time as a child and youth at church, praying and receiving the sacraments. Instead of going into the trades, Romero turned his energy toward the church and its ministries, attended seminary, was ordained into the Roman Catholic priesthood, and rose through the ranks of ecclesiastical administration, first as an assistant to a bishop, then a bishop, and ultimately being elevated to Archbishop of El Salvador. While Romero lived simply and gave generously, he also felt at home among El Salvador's wealthy and powerful elite. He was a good administrator, and, at the time, he believed that faithful stewardship involved maintaining positive relationships with wealthy donors. He had not yet discovered

---

2. Howard Thurman, *Jesus and the Disinherited* (Boston: Beacon Press, 1996), 1–2.

that morality involves just and equitable social structures as well as individual acts of kindness.

At the time Romero became a bishop and then archbishop, nearly all of El Salvador's wealth was concentrated in the hands of fourteen families, who provided significant financial support to the church, with the implicit expectation that the church would support the economic and political status quo. Any challenge to their wealth and power was met with violence and incarceration. The *campesinos,* most of whom were Indian farm laborers, lived in poverty and servitude. The church promised a heavenly reward for those who shared in the sacraments, worked hard, and were politically docile. Although El Salvador's oligarchs perpetrated violence through poverty, economic injustice, and physical threat, the church sided against the poor whenever the workers sought to challenge the status quo either through political, economic, or, failing at that, violent protest. Violence takes many forms, but perhaps the most nefarious is white-collar violence, which destroys thousands of lives by a stroke of a pen that closes a plant to insure a good financial return for shareholders or by policies that destroy the environment and put the health of millions at risk. The wealthy of El Salvador practiced subtle and indirect violence, hiring killers—even priest killers—while keeping their hands clean.

When Romero was appointed Archbishop of El Salvador, the politically active members of the priesthood were disappointed, assuming he would turn a deaf ear to the cries of the poor. In contrast, the wealthy applauded the decision, assuming he would support their interests or perhaps look the other way, if they contributed to the coffers of the church. Both groups expected that Romero would maintain the status quo in terms of the church's involvement in political and economic change. Both groups were amazed when instead Romero's eyes were opened, awakening him to God's presence in the cries of the poor and God's suffering in the pain of the disinherited. As the pastor of the people, who sought reconciliation through compassionate actions,

Romero discovered that being a faithful pastor called him to support the interests of the poor and vulnerable over the wealthy and powerful.

Following in the footsteps of Amos, Hosea, Micah, and Isaiah, Romero realized that faithfulness to God's calling required profound social critique and economic transformation. Romero experienced what Abraham Joshua Heschel described as the "divine pathos," the voice of God in the voiceless, the pain of God in those who suffer, the powerlessness of God in the disenfranchised, and the resurrection of God's realm through willingness to suffer with and on behalf of the lost, lonely, and vulnerable. The one who had been the choice of the wealthy now became their greatest critic. They sought to silence his voice, discredit his ministry, and strip him of ecclesiastical power. His life was in constant danger, and yet rather than backing down, Romero chose the way of the cross, willingly risking his life for the resurrection of the poor. The wealthy and powerful, including many in the Roman Catholic hierarchy, sought to undermine his work. They critiqued what they believed to be his left-wing orientation and politicization of the faith. Yet, for Romero, the spiritual was ultimately political. Spirituality is incarnational, immersing us in the messiness of corporate decisions and policies that redress injustices. The poor need food for their bodies as well as their spirits. The poor were the glory of God, who sought to raise them up by overturning those for whom the lure of profit supplanted the voices of the prophets.

On March 24, 1980, Romero was gunned down as he was celebrating the Eucharist, the meal of suffering, thanksgiving, and transformation. In that moment, he became "the good shepherd who sacrificed his life for his flock."[3] Like Martin Luther King Jr., Romero anticipated martyrdom. He believed that God's cause

---

3. Marie Dennis, Renny Golden, and Scott Wright, *Oscar Romero: Reflections on His Life and Writings* (Maryknoll, NY: Orbis Books, 2000), 11.

would live on and that his spirit would rise, by God's grace, in the life of the people.

THE MYSTIC AS SOCIAL REFORMER

Romero discovered that our encounters with God are profoundly relational. Authentic spirituality involves "looking at God and from God at one's neighbor or brother or sister, and an awareness that 'whatever you did to one of these, you did to me.'"[4] The transcendent God, the creator of the galaxies, is also the intimate God, who suffers with those who experience injustice and rejoices with those who experience liberation. The mystic discovers that God speaks through every event and every person, most especially the poor. This is a consistent theme among the mystics we've encountered: God experiences the pain of the world, and our intimacy with God increases our intimacy with the poor and vulnerable.

All things can be vehicles of revelation, inspiring gradual transformation or sudden Damascus Road conversions such as Romero experienced after the murder of his friend and colleague Rutilio Grande. While we may close our eyes during times of prayer and meditation, our solitary prayers find fulfillment when we open our eyes with insight and empathy, and when our praying draws us closer to the divinity hidden, and often abused and oppressed, in every person. Sensitivity, not apathy, is the fruit of mystical experience. While we may draw away from the bustling crowd and its demands in our daily meditations and regular times of retreat, the drawing away ultimately plunges us back into the world of suffering and injustice with a deeper commitment to being God's companions in healing the earth and its people. We must also pray with our hands, feet, votes, and phone calls.

---

4. Oscar Romero, *The Violence of Love* (Maryknoll, NY: Orbis Books, 2004), 1.

THE DIGNITY OF GOD'S PEOPLE

Romero experienced the poor as God's prophets. In the voice of the voiceless, he heard God's voice. Building on Irenaeus's affirmation that the glory of God is a fully alive human, Romero proclaimed that the glory of God is found in the fully alive *campesino,* the fully alive people of God daily experiencing poverty and oppression. God's presence is universal, and all things reflect God's glory, yet the poor are uniquely representative of divine revelation. The poor recognize their dependence on God, and in so doing call us toward blessed communities of justice.

God's preferential option for, and unique presence among, the poor and dispossessed does not exclude the wealthy from God's loving care and challenge. Romero preached conversion and salvation for the poor and the wealthy alike. The poor need to be uplifted by justice seeking that would require the wealthy to sacrifice their largesse. Conversely, the wealthy will save their souls by downward mobility and identification with the poor. The poor need to discover their dignity as God's beloved children. The wealthy need to discover their solidarity with the forgotten and oppressed even as they confess their sins, often unintentional and based on privilege, against the poor. God's sacraments are in the world as well as in the church. We share in the bread of life so that we might all eat together at God's table of salvation.

Romero's faith echoes Mary's Magnificat. When God comes to us, God calls us to transformed visions and behaviors. When Christ is born in us, we praise God and commit ourselves to social justice:

> My soul magnifies the Lord,
>   and my spirit rejoices in God my Savior,
>   for he has looked with favor on the lowliness
>   of his servant.

Surely, from now on all generations will call me blessed;
    for the Mighty One has done great things for me,
    and holy is his name.
His mercy is for those who fear him
    from generation to generation.
He has shown strength with his arm;
    he has scattered the proud in the thoughts
      of their hearts.
He has brought down the powerful from their thrones,
    and lifted up the lowly;
he has filled the hungry with good things,
    and sent the rich away empty.

                                (Luke 1:46–53)

God's image is our deepest reality. The *imago dei* challenges us to a mysticism of reverence and healing. Knowing the divine presence in all people, the mystic discovers that "whoever tortures a human being, whoever abuses a human being, whoever outrages a human being abuses God's image."[5] True prayer is characterized by compassionate concern for those who suffer. "The guarantee of prayer is not in saying a lot of words. The guarantee of one's petition is very easy to know: how do I treat the poor? Because that is where God is."[6]

SALVATION IN HISTORY

The authors of a reflection on Romero's life and ministry explore the meaning of spirituality in the daily lives of those El Salvadorans who accompanied Romero in the quest for justice. *"Mistica,"* or spirituality, "points to the invisible bond that unites people with each other. . . . *Mistica* is the spirit of community." Accordingly,

---

5. Ibid., 26.
6. Ibid., 35.

"*Mistica* has everything to do with history. . . . *Mistica* reveals the extraordinary in the ordinary events of history. *Mistica* requires not so much individual listening to the God within, but an attention to the voice of God revealed in the cries and whispers of the poor in our midst."[7] According to Romero, "God saves in history. Each person's life, each one's history is the meeting place God comes to."[8]

The mystic sees traces of divine guidance in every moment and encounter. This life, this place of struggle, this environment of injustice and broken dreams, is where God speaks to us. With our eyes open in prayer, Romero counseled, "Let's not meditate upon a word that is disincarnated from reality."[9] The promise of salvation is here and now as we bring our experiences of heaven, of divine inspiration, to places of wretchedness and abandonment. "We must save not the soul of the person at the hour of death but the person living in history."[10]

Salvation is this-worldly as well as beyond the grave. Romero notes that "some people want to keep a gospel so disembodied that it doesn't get involved at all in the world it must save. Christ is now in history. Christ is in the womb of the people. Christ is now bringing about a new heaven and a new earth."[11] Christ was embedded in his history as an oppressed working-class Jew who "continues to become incarnate in everyone."[12]

Mysticism embeds us in economic, social, governmental, and religious structures that can harm as well as heal. While spirituality is often a solitary enterprise, it is also a social reality that emerges from and shapes the communities to which we belong.

---

7. Dennis et al., *Oscar Romero*, 71–72.
8. Romero, *The Violence of Love*, 73.
9. Ibid., 53.
10. Ibid., 4.
11. Ibid., 102.
12. Ibid.

Accordingly, "we need communities of conversion as well as transformed persons."[13]

GOD AS COMPANION OF THE POOR AND
CHALLENGER OF THE WEALTHY

The philosopher Alfred North Whitehead described God as the
"fellow sufferer who understands."[14] Romero would have affirmed
Whitehead's sentiment. When we hear the cries of the poor, we
experience God's pain. When we hear celebrations of liberation,
we delight in God's joy. An empathetic God inspires an empathetic
spirituality and ethics. An apathetic God, distant and untouched
by the world, inspires escapist and disembodied spiritualities for
whom involvement in the complexities and messiness of social
transformation detracts from our spiritual growth. In contrast to
images of divine distance and disengagement, Romero proclaims
that the Holy One "is not a distant God—transcendent, yes,
infinite, but a God close at hand here on earth."[15] God converses
with us, guiding and listening, and "to pray is to converse with
God."[16] Deep prayer is an immersion in the historical realities that
shape millions of lives. My prayer life must include the millions of
undocumented workers, many of whom have lived in the United
States for decades contributing to our economy, who are being
threatened with deportation by our nation's current immigration
policies. My prayer life also must include the DACA children who
have lived most of their lives in the United States and who see the
United States as their home but whose ability to stay in our nation
is now at risk. My prayers must be for wise leadership among our
nation's leaders in responding to global climate change. Authentic

---

13. Ibid., 98.
14. Alfred North Whitehead, *Process and Reality: Corrected Edition*
(New York: Free Press, 1979), 351.
15. Romero, *The Violence of Love*, 136.
16. Ibid., 68.

prayer involves the sighs too deep for words emerging from my own spiritual depths; it also involves listening to God's prayers for the poor, abandoned, lonely, and oppressed welling up from within my own spirit.

"We all have a church within ourselves, our own consciousness," which inspires us to pray "with God's Spirit inside us and sharing God's life."[17] From Romero's perspective, our awareness of God's inspiration calls each of us, but most particularly the poor of the earth, to be "God's microphone," "messenger," and "prophet."[18]

God speaks to us in all things. Yet God is beyond all things, judging all human endeavor. Prophetic mysticism is both within and beyond the institutional structures of her or his nation. The prophetic mystic is profoundly iconoclastic, based on her or his experience of God's judgment on every social and political movement, including those with which he or she identifies. God's solidarity with the poor compels us constantly to "listen" to God's pain within their experiences of injustice and deprivation, challenge our own unconscious privilege, and respond with healing hearts and hands, not from above but as partners with the poor in healing the world. Our involvement in changing the world aligns us with God's realm in our time and enables us to experience holiness in the midst of struggle. "Every effort to better society, especially when injustice and sin are so ingrained, is an effort that God blesses, that God wants, that God demands of us."[19]

Reflection: Conversion of the Heart

Óscar Romero heard God's voice in the cries of the poor and dispossessed. Romero believed that the poor of the earth are God's

---

17. Ibid., 68–69.
18. Ibid., 142.
19. Ibid., 206.

prophets speaking directly to persons of status and property. He challenged the privileged to pay attention to the voices of the voiceless. In listening, we may experience a conversion of heart and commit ourselves to embodying the words of the prophet Amos to "let justice roll down like waters, and righteousness like an ever-flowing stream" (Amos 5:24) and discover prophetic practices for our time.

1. *Prayerfully examine your economic and racial privilege and that of those around you, opening to greater solidarity with persons who are vulnerable and impoverished.*
2. *Meditate on passages from the prophetic writings, such as those found in the prophet Amos. (Focus daily on the following passages: Amos 5:4–13; 5:14–17; 5:18–24; 6:1–8; 8:1–11; and 9:11–15, as well as the whole text.)*
3. *Prayerfully reflect on ways you can learn about and address poverty and powerlessness in your community.*
4. *Prayerfully consider what religious or nonreligious groups you might join to support creative social and environmental change.*

Romero spoke of the poor as the prophets of the land. In listening to the poor, we hear God's voice, speaking in sighs too deep for words and breaking down our feelings of apathy and separation. Many of us have little exposure to persons experiencing poverty, homelessness, and addiction in our own communities. We are unaware that persons are treated differently in the legal system and in their encounters with law enforcement officers as a result of race and economics. In our ignorance of history and the justice system, many assume that "liberty and justice for all" equally applies to everyone. We need a conversion of heart that will open our eyes to injustice and then lead to transformed values, behaviors, and political involvement. We need to realize that the institutions that protect us often harm those at the margins of society.

Action

Study can be a form of prayer when it alerts you to God's call to seek justice. Try intentionally exploring digital and media information related to poverty, injustice, and immigration. If you haven't already done so, learn about the experiences of undocumented immigrants, persons of color, the homeless, and people living in poverty. Take time to leave your comfort zone by volunteering at a soup kitchen, a center that helps young mothers, or a program that responds to poverty among the elderly. Listen closely and prayerfully to the news and to the words of politicians. Listen for coded language in political speeches and communications, Facebook memes, and Tweets that promote racism or political policies that support a preferential option for the wealthy. Prayerfully ask God to guide you to see holiness in the faces of refugees, mothers on welfare, children receiving free school lunches, homeless veterans and persons experiencing mental illness, and families torn apart by unemployment and addiction. Let God direct your words and steps in addressing injustice, racism, and intolerance.

Prayer of Awareness and Transformation

God of justice and mercy, whose love encompasses all creation and every person, give me hands that heal, a heart that loves, and a spirit that embraces all of your children, regardless of race, ethnicity, nation of origin, economics, and gender. Let me be a force for justice in my relationships and community involvement. In Christ's name. Amen.

12

*Something Beautiful for God:
Mother Teresa*

The mystics we have studied in this book are not afraid to get their hands dirty. They soar to the heavens in ecstasy and then plunge back to earth, committed to challenging unjust social structures. The planet is in crisis: leaders seem clueless as to how to respond to issues of environmental destruction and the growing gap between the rich and the poor. Indeed, some seem hellbent on preferring profits over God's prophetic vision. We need big visions and great hearts to respond courageously to the evils we encounter. Committed to fulfilling our vocation as God's partners in healing the earth, we must trust that God has the final word over history and that word will be grace.

Mother Teresa of Calcutta, now St. Teresa, provides spiritual inspiration for the living of these days, when national leaders and citizens speak of building walls, privilege wealth over justice, and close their ears to the cries of the poor. The future of the planet does not lie behind gated communities but in bridges of solidarity and empathy with those who suffer poverty and neglect. Mysticism expands our sense of compassion so that the cries of the poor become God's cry within us, calling us to share in their suffering and the suffering of Jesus, and provide comfort and affirmation to the "least of these."

Mother Teresa—like Albert Schweitzer—became a celebrity in her own time. Although she, like Schweitzer, with whom she

also shared a common affirmation of our vocation to share Christ
with the earth's most vulnerable people, used her celebrity status
to serve God's mission, she bore the burden and the scrutiny that
comes from operating on the world's stage. After her death, publi-
cation of her letters revealed that she lived with a sense of depression, of divine darkness, during the time of her greatest celebrity.
To scoffers, such revelations rendered her spiritual experiences
inauthentic. But to the wise observer, the fact that she soldiered
on, wearing a smile as she greeted the dying, represents the deepest
of spiritual gifts. The quality of our faith is not based fully on our
emotional lives, our moment-to-moment feelings, but on our allegiance to our calling and to the One who has called us. As Mother
Teresa herself said, "Thank God we don't serve God with our feelings—Otherwise I don't know where I would be. Pray for me."[1]

As I pondered Mother Teresa's faithfulness during her deep
spiritual depression and experiences of divine absence, the hymn
"I Have Decided to Follow Jesus" kept surfacing in my mind.

> I have decided to follow Jesus,
> I have decided to follow Jesus,
> I have decided to follow Jesus,
> No turning back no turning back. . . .
> The world behind me, the cross before me,
> The world behind me, the cross before me,
> The world behind me, the cross before me,
> No turning back, no turning back.

Despite our inner uncertainties, when we turn our lives over to
Jesus, following our call, we will find solace in the darkest valley.
With Mother Teresa, who was guided by Paul's affirmation in Gal
2:20, "It is no longer I who live, but Christ who lives in me," we

---

1. Mother Teresa, *Come Be My Light: The Private Writings of the
Saint of Calcutta* (New York: Doubleday, 2007), 255.

can let God's love flow through us to others, bringing healing one person at a time.

A Simple Calling

E. F. Schumacher once asserted that small is beautiful. Certainly, this was the case with Mother Teresa. Born with the name Anjezë Gonxhe Bojaxhiu in 1910, in the predominantly Serbian town of Skopje, Kosovo, as an adult she was under five feet in height, though from the beginning she possessed a great spirit. Her father, an advocate of Albanian statehood, died unexpectedly in 1919, leaving the family impoverished. But like my own father's family—my father was also born in 1910—Mother Teresa's family might have used the phrase "we weren't poor, we just didn't have any money" to describe their family situation. The family virtually lived in the church. Despite their financial straits, her mother instilled in her three children the spirit of gospel generosity. According to Mother Teresa, "she taught us to love God and to love our neighbor." She also counseled them to "never eat a single mouthful unless you are sharing with others."[2] At twelve, she felt the first stirrings of a vocation in religious life, which came to fruition six years later when she became part of the Loreto community in India. There she chose the name Mary Teresa of the Child Jesus.

From the beginning of her novitiate training, Mother Teresa felt an affinity with Thérèse of Lisieux, God's "little flower." Both women were the youngest of their family, were coddled in childhood, lost a parent as children, and suffered from ill health. Like Thérèse, Mother Teresa sought to do ordinary things with love, guided by her own motto, "Do something beautiful for God." Although she delighted in her calling as a teacher, she felt as if God was calling her to something more, and indeed in her late

---

2. Kerry Walters, *St. Teresa: Mystic and Missionary* (Cincinnati, OH: Franciscan Media, 2016), 2.

thirties, she experienced what she described as a "call within a call."

On September 10, 1946, she experienced what she would refer to as "a day of inspiration," guiding her to leave the Sisters of Loreto to serve the poorest of the poor, first on the streets of Calcutta and then across the globe. As Mother Teresa expresses it, "In quiet, intimate prayer with our Lord, I heard distinctly, a call within a call."[3] For the next several months, she continued to hear Jesus's voice addressing her as his "little one," and urging her to "Come, be my light." She experienced Jesus's thirst on the cross and recognized this same thirst in the forgotten poor and dying of Calcutta. According to Mother Teresa, "I felt that God wanted from me something more. He wanted me to be poor with the poor."[4] In 1948, she took off her Loreto habit, replacing it with a simple sari, white with blue stripes, which she hoped would be the habit of the order that would emerge from God's call to her. After taking six months of medical training, she began serving the poorest of the poor, dying beggars on the streets and members of the untouchable class.

Her work with the dying inspired her to create a home for the dying, where people of all faiths could be spiritually midwifed and physically comforted as they took the next steps in their journey from earth to heaven. Accused of trying to convert Hindus, Mother Teresa responded:

> I do convert . . . I do convert you to be a better Hindu, a
> better Catholic, a better Muslim, or Jain or Buddhist. I
> would like to help you to find God. When you find Him,
> it is up to you to do what you want with him.[5]

---

3. Ibid., 26.
4. Ibid., 27–29.
5. Ibid., 43.

The point of her work was simply to share God's love with those in need, recognizing that as we give to the poor and dying, we learn from them. In Jesus's path, there is no ultimate separation between giver and receiver. We are all God's beloved and needy children, vulnerable and dependent, blessed and loved.

> We want them to feel that they are wanted. . . . We want them to know that there are people who really love them, who really want them, at least for the few hours they have to live, to know human and divine love.[6]

For the next forty years, Mother Teresa sought simply to love. Even during her own dark night of the soul, she let go of her own feelings of abandonment so that God's love could flow through her to the lost and forgotten. Mysticism is, for her, the gift of communion with God and all God's children. Even after she received the Nobel Peace Prize in 1979 and a year later the Barat Ratna, or Jewel of India, the highest honor an Indian citizen can receive, she remained humble, believing herself to be a simple instrument of God, following wherever Jesus led and doing whatever he commanded.

In her final years, Mother Teresa saw the face of God in persons dying of AIDS. Scorned by friends and family, judged as sinners by those who presumed themselves to be righteous, they were to Mother Teresa simply God's beloved children, for whom our Savior died and with whom our Savior suffers.

Mother Teresa died in 1997 and was canonized as St. Teresa in 2016. Shortly before beginning her work in the slums, Mother Teresa dreamed that she had died. When she found herself at the gates of heaven, St. Peter turned her away, saying that there was no need of her since there were no slums in heaven. This "saint of the

---

6. Ibid.

gutter" angrily responded that she would return to heaven, filling it with the helpless and homeless.[7]

CHRIST IN HIS DISTRESSING DISGUISE

One of the key elements of the order led by Mother Teresa (the Missionaries of Charity) was to "give our whole-hearted service to the poorest of the poor—to Christ in his distressing disguise."[8] Mother Teresa's mysticism was incarnational. When Christ took flesh, he truly became embodied in our world—not just in Bethlehem and Jerusalem but in Calcutta and New York. Jesus is present in the person with AIDS, in the dying untouchable, in the immigrant anxious about being deported and immigrant children traumatized by being separated from their parents, and in the Syrian family seeking shelter from war. Jesus's suffering on the cross and his cry "I thirst" echoes across the planet, calling us to serve him in the lost, lonely, vulnerable, and forgotten.

Beneath the frightful exterior or the obnoxious demeanor, Christ is present and needs to be addressed through acts of loving kindness. God is hidden in the dying and diseased. In their eyes, we see Christ's eyes. In their pain, we feel the nails in Jesus's hands. In their hope, we can see God's quest for healing and wholeness in life's most challenging situations. Mother Teresa's vision of Christ in all things inspired her and her followers to move from apathy to empathy and from empathy to action, seeking to respond to God's presence one person at a time. While she saw the value of political action in response to poverty and sickness, Mother Teresa's calling—like that of Dorothy Day—was primarily to minister intimately and personally wherever there was a need. For Christ is

---

7. Ibid., 99.

8. Malcolm Muggeridge, *Something Beautiful for God* (San Francisco: Harper & Row, 1971), 97.

here, and the Christ in us bursts forth when we see and respond to Christ's presence in the pain experienced by others.

SOMETHING BEAUTIFUL FOR GOD

Mother Teresa, the "saint of the gutters," was inspired by Christ's invitation to experience him in all who suffer and are heavily burdened. Her counsel to her Sisters and Brothers in the Missionaries of Charity was: "Seeking the face of God in everything, everyone, and everywhere, all the time, and seeing his hand in every happening—that is contemplation in the heart of the world."[9] Experiencing the divine in all things, our calling is simply "to do something beautiful for God."[10]

Mother Teresa stressed the importance of silent prayer, of centering the spirit on God alone. Silence leads to vision—to encountering God in all things—and vision leads to action—bringing God's presence to everyone in ways that heal and affirm. The poor and vulnerable need to know, above all else, that they are loved. In loving actions, even those with little likelihood of cure or success, we bring Christ's light into the darkness of pain and loneliness.

I believe that we have choices in every situation to give God a more beautiful or uglier world. I believe that God experiences the world and that our lives shape God's experience and enhance or limit God's healing presence in the world. We are truly God's hands and heart; but more than that, we are God's companions whose loving actions bring joy to our creator's heart. Although she didn't claim to be a theologian, Mother Teresa embodied a metaphysics of love, in which God's love flows through us to others and then back again to enrich God's experience. We are blessed to be a blessing, and our blessings give joy and healing to persons in

9. Walters, *St. Teresa*, 84.
10. Ibid., 89.

distress and bring delight and beauty to God's experience of the world.

In the Darkest Valley, God Is with Us

After her experience of God's voice guiding her to a new vocation, Mother Teresa was plunged—like Thérèse of Lisieux and John of the Cross—into the dark night of the soul. In one of her letters, she describes the spiritual emptiness that hounded her days, despite her calling to be an apostle of joy to the dying and forgotten of the world.

> Tell me, Father, why is there so much pain and darkness in my soul? Sometimes I find myself saying "I can't bear it any longer" with the same breath I say "I am sorry, do with me what you wish."[11]

In another letter, the "saint of darkness," as she was described, confesses:

> They say people in hell suffer eternal pain because of the loss of God—they would go through all that suffering if they had just a little hope of possessing God. In my soul I just feel that terrible pain and loss—of God not wanting me—of God not being God—of God not really existing. (Jesus, forgive my blasphemies, I have been told to write about everything.) That darkness that surrounds me on all sides—I can't lift up my soul—No light or inspiration enters my soul.[12]

Saints and mystics—like Jesus himself—are tempted and tried as we all are. They may fall into sin and recognize their pain yet

---

11. Mother Teresa, *Come Be My Light* (New York: Doubleday, 2007), 189.

12. Ibid., 192–93.

continue following their call. Mother Teresa was clear that her faith did not depend on her feelings. There were times that she didn't even feel like praying. It was at those times she recognized that the prayers of others would sustain her faith and mission. "Thank God, we don't serve God with our feelings. Otherwise I don't know where I would be. Pray for me," she wrote to one of her spiritual advisors.[13]

Although she often felt great inner emptiness, she continued to greet the lost and forgotten of the world with a smile. She took one step at a time, giving Christ's love to the least of these and seeing Christ in others, despite her sense of Christ's absence in her own life. As every parent and faithful spouse and friend knows, love is about commitment, not how we are feeling at any given moment. Couples proclaim their love "for better or for worse; for richer or for poorer; in sickness and in health," knowing that some day they may have to endure the loving drudgery of caring for a spouse who no longer knows their name or whose day-to-day relationship is more of a burden than a joy. Mother Teresa saw herself as God's instrument and relied on God's grace to guide and energize her amid her spiritual challenges, some of which may have reflected her own identification with Christ's sufferings and the suffering of the poor. She affirmed, "I am ready to accept whatever He gives and give whatever He takes with a big smile."[14]

Like the Psalmist who proclaimed, "My God, my God, why have you forsaken me?" mystics bring their brokenness to God, seeking God's healing touch as well as the inspiration and strength to continue the journey of holiness and service. The darkness may never go away, but we can encounter divine companionship as we walk through the darkest valleys of life.

Mother Teresa's depression did not invalidate her holiness or mystical relationship with God. She continued to smile and love,

---

13. Ibid., 255.
14. Ibid., 235.

and out of that love to bring comfort to the dying. She continued to follow God's calling regardless of how she felt. The encounter with God is revealed in the daily tasks of life as much as in ecstatic experiences. Living by your vows, through all the personal and spiritual seasons of life, is also to be a witness to the One who has called us and loves us.

Reflection: Doing Something Beautiful for God

Mother Teresa found God on the streets of Calcutta. She experienced God as the deepest reality of those who had been ostracized, neglected, and left to die. Beneath apparent ugliness, she found beauty and sought to do something beautiful for God. God speaks to us in the glories of the heavens and the grandeur of the mountains. God also addresses us in the pain of the forgotten, shining through their rough exterior to reveal the light of Christ's presence. Commitment to bring beauty to God and the world is enhanced by the following spiritual practices:

1. *Commit yourself daily to do something beautiful for God.*
2. *Ask for God's vision as you seek to see holiness in persons who seem from your perspective to be the least likely to bear the divine imprint.*
3. *Practice meditation to help you maintain a still point in your busy and, at times, conflictual world.*
4. *Despite your state of mind or emotional life, do your best to keep your commitments to persons in need of your support.*

Mother Teresa vowed to be faithful to God in every situation. She saw herself as a divine pencil by which God was bringing beauty to the canvas of life. She wanted to do God's will in every life situation. We can experience divinity in ecstasy and equanimity. We also can experience God in empathy with those who suffer and conflict with forces of injustice.

Action

Throughout the day, ask God to guide you in faithfulness. "Loving God, I give my life to you. Lead me and guide me to be faithful to you. Let this moment be one in which I give your love to everyone and share my love with you in every situation. Help me to ease the pain and quench the thirst of your anguished children." Or, you might simply ask, "Guide me in this situation that I might share your love." Let these, or other words, be your vow regardless of how you feel. Obedience, not emotion, joins us with God's vision for our lives.

Prayer of Awareness and Transformation

Holy God, I vow to be your healing and loving presence in every situation. Guide me one moment at a time. Help me to be faithful to your task each moment of the day. In Christ's name. Amen.

EPILOGUE

Our Legs Are Praying:
Twenty-First-Century Mystics

As noted earlier, in reflecting on his experiences marching with Martin Luther King Jr., Abraham Joshua Heschel stated that he felt like his legs were praying. While an important characteristic of mysticism involves time spent in solitude, the mystics described in this book were always on the move spiritually and physically. God called them in moments of quiet reflection, and they also experienced God's still, small voice on the picket line, challenging national policy, standing up for workers, and serving time in the jail house. The reality in which we live and move embraces all creation, not just the cloister. Faithfulness to God awakens us to Christ, disguised in the poor, vulnerable, dying, and marginalized. God initiates the call to discipleship, and this call invites us to become God's partners in healing the earth. Mystics are "woke" people, to use the language of today's protest movements, cognizant of their complicity in injustices that most of us fail to experience and committed to challenge injustice first in themselves and then in the world.

Mystics are also "woke" to God's presence in unexpected places. The traditional doctrines of omnipresence, omniscience, and omnipotence are not academic and unrelated to the world; they shape the everyday life and commitments of mystics. The ever-present God is found in the slums of Calcutta, the African backwaters of Lambaréné, the soup kitchens of Manhattan, and the streets of Montgomery, Alabama. The all-knowing God expe-

150

riences the cries of the poor *campesino* and the silent hopelessness of the dispirited worker, and wants us to wake up to their pain and then do something about it. The ever active and compassionate God needs companions in the quest to heal the earth and challenges us to move from the study and classroom to the peace march and halls of Congress.

There is a mystic in you and everyone else, waiting to be awakened. None of the people in this text set out to be mystics or social reformers. They didn't expect to be models to others or remembered for decades to come. In many cases, they were better prepared for the classroom, monastery, pulpit, or medical theater. But God called them as God called the women and men in Galilee, and they followed, not sure at first where the path would take them and often surprised at the accolades they received for just doing the tasks that Jesus called them to.

Simone Weil, quoted earlier, asserted that in our time "It is not merely enough to be a saint, but we must have the saintliness demanded by the present moment, a new saintliness without precedent. . . . A new type of sanctity."[1] We need to be mystics of the moment, not disqualified by past behavior, imperfection, or depression, and not even disqualified by our doubts and questions. The mystics described in this book followed no common norm in lifestyle, personality, marital status, or spiritual experience. Some could be rough-hewn and ornery in their single-minded quest to bring God's realm to earth "as it is in heaven." Yet, like the geode, they experienced God beneath their own rough exteriors and discovered God in the hidden and jagged, and often scorned, persons whom God calls beloved children.

The saintliness of this unique moment calls us to wake up to the injustices of our time. Mystic vision, in our time, awakens us to a God-filled world, tarnished and threatened by human artifice.

---

1. Simone Weil, *Waiting for God* (New York: HarperCollins, 2009), 51.

God calls us today to enlarge our hearts and minds to embrace the suffering of our planet. God's call may come as you are touched by the pain of an endangered species or a photograph of a refugee child. God may speak to you as you move from serving breakfast at a soup kitchen to exploring and then responding to the social conditions and political decisions that create homelessness in the richest nation on earth. Like Peace Pilgrim, you may discover that you need to walk the talk, whether across the nation as she did or simply in another part of town to support the education of impoverished children as a tutor or as a spokesperson for justice at the Board of Education. Your encounter with God may even take you to the picket line or jail.

"It will be solved in the walking." This counsel, attributed to St. Augustine, is the calling of saintliness and mysticism in our time. It describes a spirituality on the move, widening its circle of concern and responsibility, moving from care for your own spiritual life to ensuring that others have the opportunity to deepen their spirits by challenging anything that gets in the way of people discovering the divine within.

God calls each of us to our own kind of mysticism. God made each of us unique and speaks intimately to each one of us in our life experiences, personality, social location, gifts, and encounters. God calls each of us for our time and place and not another, and though we may not know the One who calls, God reveals God's vision for us on the path we take as we follow God's guidance.

Today, we need mystics who are heavenly minded and earthly good. We need people of stature, large-hearted people with big visions of what our world would look like if we mirrored God's heavenly vision. We also need people who can translate this vision to the hardscrabble and ambiguous world of daily life, people who take time to meditate in the maelstrom and from their meditations receive guidance, compassion, and patience to respond to the seeming intractable problems of poverty, species destruction and climate change, cultural incivility, racism, and the various forms of sexism, greed, and consumerism.

You are a mystic! God is touching you, calling you, inspiring you, giving you a vocation for the world and the energy to bring forth God's vision of Shalom. Jewish mystics believe that the world is saved one person at a time. Jesus knew that without the return of the wayward sheep, the ninety-nine would also be lost. The task may seem too large and your resources too small. Yet the God of today's mystics is the God of the mustard seed and five loaves and two fish, and with our small gifts, dedicated to God, we can transform the world.

I want to conclude by reminding you of one of the anchors of this book, the words of Albert Schweitzer, who described the path of discipleship both in the first century and in our time as one of constant growth and adventure—casting nets, cooking meals, caring for children, or sitting in their offices. The "he" spoken of by Schweitzer in chapter 1 and below is Jesus of Nazareth, and it is also the divine witness that comes without sect or doctrine or even religious background or faith tradition to awaken us to our vocation to heal the earth. God is here in this place, in the world in all its tragic beauty—and now we know it!

> He comes to us as One unknown, without a name, as of old, by the lakeside, He came to those men who knew Him not. He speaks to us the same words: "Follow thou me!" and sets us to the tasks which He has to fulfill for our time. He commands. And to those who obey Him, whether they be wise or simple, He will reveal himself in the toils, the conflicts, the sufferings which they shall pass through in His fellowship, and, as an ineffable mystery, they shall learn in their own experience Who He is.[2]

---

2. Albert Schweitzer, *The Quest of the Historical Jesus* (London: A. & C. Black, 1931), 401.

Index